PRAISE FOR *BELONGING RULES*

"In *Belonging Rules*, Brad Deutser shines a light on what I consider to be one of the most important predictors of long-term success at organizations: belonging. Moreover, study after study shows that social connection is the greatest predictor of long-term happiness. So, this book highlighting belonging, authenticity, and vulnerability is at the intersection of so many crucial issues at work, at home, and in our society."

**—Shawn Achor, *New York Times* bestselling author of
the *Happiness Advantage* and *Big Potential***

"As someone who worked alongside Brad in one of the most volatile debates in collegiate athletics, I witnessed Brad engage with ALL communities and saw firsthand his humility, his compassion, and his ability to engage and connect when tensions are highest. I would urge leaders in business to implement *Belonging Rules*—Brad has done the work and has incredible insights to share."

**—Richard J. Reddick, EdD, Senior Vice Provost for Curriculum and Enrollment
and Dean of Undergraduate Studies, The University of Texas at Austin**

"The Belonging Rules help us reach a better understanding of not only ourselves, but of the teams, the missions, and the causes of which we are a part. Because at the end of the day, most of us just want to feel like we belong to something bigger than ourselves."

**—Nate Boyer, US Army Green Beret, former NFL football
player, and Cofounder, Merging Vets and Players**

"As a global business that opens the world to people and experiences, belonging is at the center of all we do. The important concepts in the book help to bring diverse people together while celebrating their differences and unique cultures."

—Lisa Lutoff-Perlo, Vice Chairman, External Affairs, Royal Carribean Group

"In a business defined by wins, football requires an unmatched level of understanding and teamwork. *Belonging Rules* fearlessly drives the kind of change leaders are not only looking for but demanding. It is a must-have leadership playbook."

—D. Cal McNair, Chairman and Chief Executive Officer, Houston Texans

"Brad Deutser expertly marries his research with real-world examples to empower leaders to build acceptance and unity in their organizations. The book's five rules challenge traditional notions, providing a road map to build a more connected, engaged, and productive workforce."

—David Eagleman, neuroscientist, bestselling author, and Guggenheim Fellow

"As someone who craves connection and also freedom and independence, the quest to find where I belong has been a lifelong journey. Brad Deutser brilliantly captures this universal human need to belong; why we need it and how to make space for it. A genuine and compelling concept, and the tangible steps to translate it into action.

—Marissa Orr, former Google and Facebook executive, and bestselling author of *Lean Out*

"Brad is a master of challenging the status quo and focusing on what is possible through exploring alternate perspectives. The journey for belonging and acceptance only starts when you open your perspective and lens to what is possible. Brad creates a map and process that focuses your attention, challenges your convictions, and produces success. It is time for you to start your journey into understanding the power of belonging."

—Derek van der Merwe, Director of Athletics, Bowling Green State University

"Brad Deutser's thinking is brave, irreverent, and inspirational. Brad is a man of unquenchable curiosity . . . intent on nudging business, our nation, and my students toward enduring solutions. His Belonging Rules have been instrumental in creating connection and commonality among a diverse group of students and entrepreneurs."

—Dave Cook, Director, Wolff Center for Entrepreneurship, Bauer College of Business

"*Belonging Rules* is a must-read for corporate America. Deutser's team has conducted thousands of interviews to gain a multidimensional understanding of belonging. Throughout the book, Deutser provides action items which will lead to measurable results."

—Dr. Laura G. Murillo, President and CEO, Houston Hispanic Chamber of Commerce

"I am constantly impressed by Brad's ability to lead difficult, often uncomfortable, conversations centered around inclusivity and belonging. He skillfully works to makes others feel heard, valued, and comfortable regardless of the topic. By implementing these Belonging Rules into my career and personal life, I have been able to successfully work through tough situations and build strong, lasting relationships."

—Logan Eggleston, Galatasaray Voleybol (Turkey) and 2023 NCAA Women's Volleyball Player of the Year

"*Belonging Rules* is an inspiring, relevant, and executable road map! Brad leverages his unique insights and acute awareness of leadership and culture to provide a one-of-a-kind framework to address society's most critical, controversial, and complex issues."

—Heath Butler, Founder, Urban Capital Network

"In *Belonging Rules*, Brad has masterfully distilled the most essential elements of belonging into actionable leadership principles. In the work we've done with Brad and his firm over the past few years, these principles have improved our culture and generated tangible results."

—Dwayne Hyzak, Chief Executive Officer, Main Street Capital Corporation

"Never has the need to belong been so important, given that some face the added challenge of proving they belong. Truly all inclusive, from the executive to the new hire, *Belonging Rules* provides the tools to establish and cultivate a culture of belonging from every perspective."

—Rick Jaramillo, Bank of America, Market Leader

"In today's divided, polarized world, it's vital that leaders bridge differences and foster genuine connection in the organizations and communities they serve. Brad Deutser offers practical, actionable tools for leaders to apply as they embark on the journey of creating and sustaining belonging. *Belonging Rules* is a must-read for leaders of today and tomorrow!"

—Dr. Mikki Hebl, Martha and Henry Malcolm Lovett Professor of Psychological Sciences and Management and Dr. Eden King, Lynette S. Autrey Professor of Psychology at Rice University, coauthors of *Working Together: The Science of DEI*

"Brad Deutser's *Belonging Rules* provides both practical and thoughtful approaches to combating ideological, institutional, interpersonal, and internalized forms of oppression rampant in workplaces today. By focusing on inclusion, Brad is helping to humanize the worker experience, critical in supporting successful organizations."

—Dr. Solange Charas, CEO, HCMoneyball; Lecturer at Columbia University; and coauthor of *Humanizing Human Capital*

"Belonging is an essential human need, and in this captivating book, Brad Deutser has beautifully captured the importance of finding one's place in the world. With a blend of personal stories, scientific research, and practical tools, this book offers a powerful exploration of the many facets of belonging. It's a must-read for anyone who has ever felt disconnected or struggled to find their place, and for those seeking to deepen their understanding of human connection. This book is a compassionate and insightful guide that will inspire readers to cultivate a sense of belonging in their own lives, businesses, teams, and communities."

—Matthew Hayes, Senior Associate Athletic Director of Internal Operations, Chief Financial Officer, University of Arizona

"Excellent! *Belonging Rules* is a groundbreaking book that empowers leaders to address the critical challenge of creating workplace belonging. Based on extensive research, Brad Deutser creates the ultimate guide to equip leaders with the confidence to navigate the complexities of the modern workforce."

—Marshall Goldsmith, *Thinkers50* #1 Executive Coach and *New York Times* bestselling author of *The Earned Life*, *Triggers*, and *What Got You Here Won't Get You There*

ALSO BY BRAD DEUTSER

Leading Clarity

BELONGING RULES

Five Crucial Actions That Build
Unity and Foster Performance

BRAD DEUTSER

Matt Holt Books
An Imprint of BenBella Books, Inc.
Dallas, TX

Matt Holt is an imprint of BenBella Books, Inc.
10440 N. Central Expressway
Suite 800
Dallas, TX 75231
benbellabooks.com
Send feedback to feedback@benbellabooks.com

BenBella and *Matt Holt* are federally registered trademarks.

Printed in the United States of America
10 9 8 7 6 5 4 3 2 1

Library of Congress Control Number: 2023004598
ISBN 9781637744024 (hardcover)
ISBN 9781637744031 (electronic)

Copyediting by James Fraleigh
Proofreading by Jenny Bridges and Marissa Wold Uhrina
Indexing by WordCo Indexing Services, Inc.
Text design and composition by Aaron Edmiston
Cover design by Christy Barthelme Blackburn and Julie Zaugg
Printed by Lake Book Manufacturing

Special discounts for bulk sales are available.
Please contact bulkorders@benbellabooks.com.

To everyone who believes in the magical power of belonging—
which, for me, starts with Jill, Ashley, Andrew, my parents,
family, colleagues, and friends. Pure gratitude.

CONTENTS

AN INVITATION INSIDE

L et's start with the obvious. Why am I even in the conversation, much less an expert, on the topic of belonging in organizations? It is a fair question and one that I face squarely throughout this book. From interactions with leaders and people across the globe to my unique life experiences, I have found that it takes all of us to create a space for the necessary conversations and actions that facilitate what it really means to belong. The time of workarounds or intentionally bypassing individuals, groups, divisive topics, and difficult conversations is in the past.

I may appear at first glance to be an odd vessel for the topic of belonging and its message. I am often put in situations where someone in the conversation states, "You don't belong here." It is not a one-time occurrence; it's become a seemingly all-the-time conversation. And, in my line of business with the heated rhetoric and complexity of today's business environment, perhaps it is not a surprise. Far too often, the conversation devolves, before it even starts, into a discussion of the obvious—my age, gender, race, perceived privilege, or any other surface attribution. My qualifications or desire to make a difference easily get pushed aside or are quickly overlooked by the people already in the discussions who believe that only others like them could possibly understand their perspective. When that occurs, we invariably reach a crossroads where we can agree that people can stay stuck talking about the surface elements that are obvious to the human eye—or that the conversation can evolve (and it must) to substantive issues that we can debate, challenge, and make progress on. These crossroads often appear as a diversity-driven conversation, but instead it is, in every sense, a leadership conversation.

Given the research-validated outcomes and demonstrated financial impact belonging offers, organizations should make cultivating belonging a personal leadership imperative across the world. It is the future of business and the key determinant of whether a leader will remain one as well as how effective that leader will be in that role. Belonging is the antidote to many of the most pressing issues organizations of all shapes, sizes, and varieties now face. It allows leaders to recalibrate their approach to shift diversity, equity, and inclusion to a supportive position as a part of a more holistic belonging equation. This shift mitigates the politics of DEI and goes to the heart of human leadership. Belonging cannot remain an afterthought. It is a crucial component that sits at the top of what is needed for cohesion in organizations and groups of all kinds, and it is a lever that leaders can pull to enact desirable, necessary, and unifying change in their organizations and their communities.

Every day, we see the challenges that the ongoing outcry for inclusion is causing. It is a noisy factor exacerbating the disconnect that has invaded the business environment. We are seeing workforces growing restless because people do not feel like they fit the same as they did before or because they are hesitant to stand up, speak out, or act out for fear of retribution from a supervisor—or worse, ostracization from coworkers and friends in the community. This collective workforce anxiety impacts everything. Safety. Happiness. Performance. Longevity. Resilience. Connection. Positivity. Health and well-being. Unity. And it is one of the great and silent dangers that is lurking deep within the walls of business. The disconnect with how people see themselves and their company and how they find their fit is at the heart of this book and our exploration on leadership and belonging.

THE MOST IMPORTANT PREDICTOR

Most leaders think about belonging as yet another squishy, amorphous concept more easily relegated to Human Resources than as a function under the vision, direction, and responsibility of the C-suite. Our work and research in this space says emphatically, "No!" My firm's research team, including industrial-organizational and cognitive psychologists in our Clarity Institute and Institute for Belonging, surveyed more than fifteen thousand employees across varied industries and occupational roles, finding not only that belonging is a critical determinant of employee job satisfaction, engagement, and effort but also that it is the *most important* predictor of these outcomes. Belonging predicts job satisfaction, engagement, and effort over and above employees' perceptions of organizational culture or strategy. Think about belonging as the bedrock of organizational performance and employee commitment.

Yet leaders often focus on traditional or historically measured business issues, ignoring the importance of belonging. No more. Numerous research studies that we have conducted prove that while measuring affinity for any number of organizational or DEI issues is valuable, that affinity will not shift organizational performance and outcomes more than that for belonging. Interestingly, and counter to conventional thinking, belonging has a greater impact on employee retention than does compensation. Compensation is a moving target and, as such, a temporary offering. The sense of belonging is more lasting, with a deeper connection and motivation for employees to stay with the company. People will leave their jobs if they feel like they don't belong there. Belonging creates a workplace where people feel included, accepted, safe, and valued. For leaders, belonging is the sustainable solution for employee engagement and retention. This is not a pass-down-the-organization want-to-have; it has become the must-have, the must-measure, and the must-excel-at imperative for every leader up and down and across every organization.

Our research delves deep into human behavior and how people understand, adopt, and value belonging—especially in the workplace. It also highlights the ways in which belonging can be promoted and strengthened in various settings, including within companies, groups, and teams anywhere in the world. The research suggests that belonging is a fundamental driver of human motivation and key to unlocking greater performance, resilience, and a willingness to challenge one's existing perspectives.

THE CALL FOR BELONGING

Through our research, teaching, and consulting work on this topic, we have interviewed and worked with thousands of individuals. When asked what belonging means to them, each person has a different way of describing it and how they work to attain it. One thing that most responses have in common is an increasing desire for belonging in both one's personal and business spaces. This is what belonging means to me and how we define it in our work:

> Belonging is where we hold space for something of shared importance. It is where we come together on values, purpose, and identity; a space of acceptance where agreement is not required but a shared framework is understood; where there is an invitation into the space; an intentional choice to take part in; something vital to a sense of connection, security, and acceptance.

Belonging must be something that each of us, as individuals and leaders, recognizes is available to us. In many ways, it is that open invitation people crave. It is meant to be such a part of our everyday lives that we often overlook its power and influence on our attitudes and actions. Yet, even when we find it, we are never fully settled in belonging. As attitudes and opinions rapidly evolve, it is something we work for and work toward—regardless of our age, our environment, or the place we occupy.

Yet, belonging extends so far beyond business. It is essential to the human psyche and a fundamental human need. As humans, we are motivated to connect and affiliate with others. Overall, research on belonging has provided a deeper comprehension of the importance of social connections and group membership for human well-being and functioning. For young children, it may present a choice that paves the trajectory for their lives—between belonging to the Boys & Girls Club or belonging to a gang. For an athlete, the locker room creates a unique place for most to belong, and in the elite, high-performing teams, for all to belong. It takes work and courage from the leader, the individual, and the organization. But belonging must be understood, embraced, and actualized in each of our own unique ways. When it is delegated or left for someone else to initiate, we often lose our standing and our ability to design a space for ourselves and others.

BEING ON THE OUTSIDE

Each of us can identify times in our lives when we have questioned, "Do I belong?" I am not exempt. I have been told, with words and actions, how and where I belong. My leadership journey is littered with incredible stories of human connection and disconnection. I am the proud grandson of immigrants who worked hard to become Americans and fit in. I was the kid (nerd) in the back of the middle-school classroom—ignored and overlooked. Later in life, I was told by members of a club I was trying to get into that "we aren't ready for people like you." People like me? I work with some of the top leaders in the world, yet something about me—in this case, my religion—stood out and made "me" the exception to "them." And not the right kind of exception.

What increasingly became clear to me is that it isn't up to other people to determine where I belong. Belonging is a personal choice. My journey as a leader has taught me how to create space where I can not only fit but also thrive. My journeys have allowed me the unique vantage point to explore the topic of inclusion and consider the complexity of it from inside and outside the role of leadership. What we now know is that belonging is the critical leadership element for all that comes next, and that when it is incorporated into the DNA of the organization, it becomes the most impactful and lasting determinant of success for the leader today.

The fact is that if we all take time to reflect, we share similar stories—albeit at different extremes—of being on the outside. We all can remember times we either pushed people or left them on the outside of something at some point in our lives. This awareness of our humanness is at the core of belonging, and it belongs to each of us—regardless of our socioeconomic status, our race, our religion, our sexual orientation, or our job title.

TACKLING EXPLOSIVE ISSUES

As a consultant and coach, I work in places most people feel uncomfortable in and try to avoid, and I'm often thrust into the heart of vitriolic, hateful, and challenging conversations where there is rarely one answer. I have seen the best and worst of leadership. I work with and through complex, organizationally draining, and racially, politically, and societally charged issues with the aim of bringing together diverse perspectives and people. I am known for fearlessly questioning things that need to be examined and seeking 100% of the truth. I work to initiate constructs, both physically and figuratively, that expand leadership in a more human, connective way. It is in these spaces and conversations where I find that I get as much as I give—learning from the different experiences and viewpoints of every participant in the room. I embrace this give-and-take, the exchange of different and often opposing ideas, viewpoints, and experiences, as central to fostering belonging in organizations.

I was struck at the end of an all-female workshop where each participant identified herself as being part of a minority or disenfranchised group (Black, Asian, Hispanic, or LGBTQ+) when one of the participants shared her "positive takeaway" from the experience: "I didn't know before today that white men could ever face similar problems women of color have. I thought you had it easy. I cannot believe how much we actually have in common as leaders." The conversation continued, and it became clear that her view was shared by many others in the session. The power of our work together came at that moment when we broke through the stereotypes—women, men, white, brown, black, wealthy, poor, straight, gay, and on and on. It is when we allow ourselves to be vulnerable and offer a glimpse of who we really are that we often find that we share something more powerful than the differences that divide us.

It is why this book is designed to offer a framework for new thinking where we examine the most difficult topics in a way that focuses on collaboration, optimism, reverence, and respect, all joined with suggested approaches, actions, and ways to get to deeper explorations. We intentionally challenge conventional thought and, at times, uncomfortably go against the most current grain of thinking. It is never to be disrespectful; rather, we want to give space to challenge what we are told or made to believe is right, from one extreme to the other. This is intentional so that you can form, in a safe space, your own opinions and decisions on how you will lead in a world that is dictating what is and what is not acceptable. This book provides leaders with a proven pathway to encourage dialogue and allow diverse perspectives to be delivered, heard, evaluated, and acted upon. It is a call to leaders to inspire a shift in their organizations and their lives—a shift that bridges differences and divisions. This book will teach you how to courageously approach contentious issues in a way that stops pushing people out and starts pulling them in. That invitation inside is core to how we will change the future of our businesses and society.

It is leaders who must create community and rebuild the foundation upon which meaningful, authentic relationships can rest. This requires an intentional change of focus, clearing a path to understanding, acceptance, generosity, and goodwill. This is a human issue and one that will define the workplace for generations to come. Success will undoubtedly be delivered by and through those who create capacity for belonging.

SOMETHING GREATER THAN OURSELVES

I have been at the center of hundreds of DEI and ESG initiatives, as well as complex social issues with NFL and NCAA football teams, major universities, collegiate athletic programs, high-profile entertainment companies, media outlets, energy companies, aviation companies, financial institutions, healthcare giants, and nonprofit organizations. In each case, leaders were tasked with—and accepted—the challenge of building solution sets with various choices, models for making decisions, and broader systems to include multiple and diverse perspectives. Each time, they answered the challenge by leveraging the rules and unifying power of belonging.

To help leaders at all levels create the space necessary for belonging, there are basic principles that I have found to be highly effective. I call these principles the Belonging Rules. These are the five things that leaders and contributors at every level of any organization must consider every time they make decisions for themselves, their people, and their company. The Belonging Rules are for everyone and can be an important navigational tool when applied to the complexity of both our times and the every day.

The Belonging Rules

1. **Turn into the power.** Meet the demand for direct and intentional forays into the heart of power structures, forces, and accepted traditions.
2. **Listen without labels.** Hear what is spoken without judgment while engaging the unspoken with humanity and heart.
3. **Choose identity over purpose.** Create an ecosystem that recognizes both the complexity as well as the wholeness of identity, which defines the space for inclusion.
4. **Challenge everything.** Promote an open environment for inquiry, free of conflict, devoid of oppositional energy, and driven by a positive spirit of curiosity.
5. **Demand 100% of the truth.** Reject the more typical 80% of the truth in modern business, and instead require 100% of the truth 100% of the time.

Belonging Rules takes the narrative further by placing individual leadership and organizational identity at the heart of what continues as an imperative. Backed by research, interviews with current leaders working in real time through the most pressing issues, as well as insider access to successful executives in high-profile companies and institutions, this book provides leaders at all levels not only the permission but also the backbone and tools to redesign the basics of leading in any environment to incorporate today's business essential, *belonging*. It challenges readers with practical exercises, thought-provoking questions, and inspiring stories that illustrate the connection between belonging, self-direction, interconnectedness, and success. Together, the lessons and stories in this book conclusively demonstrate that success is incumbent on a leader's ability to build the capacity for human belonging.

Throughout this book, we work to

- unpack existing power structures,
- address evolving leadership and management issues,
- discuss how to redefine the relationship with diverse stakeholders,
- dissect how to properly evaluate how an organization contributes to today's social economy,
- balance the health of the people providing whole-being wellness with the needs and demands of the work itself, and
- prepare talent for contribution and enthusiastic participation as part of a greater understanding and, yes, greater belonging.

THE HUMAN LEADER

Belonging Rules is about bringing forward the best of what it means to be human in this complex, volatile, and changing time. It is about being a more human leader—for yourself and those you serve. To me, this is where the conversation and action must evolve: away from the divisiveness of individual differences and headfirst into a space where differences are encouraged, discussed, debated, and acted upon. All of this is necessary in a space of belonging. And it starts with you.

So, as you read, allow yourself to be challenged. Allow yourself to be right and wrong at the same time. Allow yourself to explore not just your beliefs but also your leadership and the opportunities it presents to you and others. Allow yourself to be open to growth and evolution—that is where belonging often begins. Invite others into your space, your ideas, your world. And allow yourself to be invited into others' spaces.

Yes, you may leave yourself vulnerable and exposed, but isn't that at the foundation of the greatest, most powerful leaders? Your courage will be rewarded with the richness and diversity of the spaces you create and the relationships you make along the way.

Chapter 1

BECOMING COMFORTABLE WITH THE UNCOMFORTABLE

Belonging Rule #1: **TURN INTO THE POWER**

L et's face it: talking about race, gender, politics, religion, and other traditional structures is not for the timid leader—but they *are* topics for today's leader. Because any difference between people can now become a flashpoint, leaders are expected to expertly navigate through the tension.

The natural human tendency is to stay on the sidelines, to encircle oneself with people who reinforce our worldview—or to avoid the conflict altogether. Yet, conflict is everywhere, and it seems hard for people to get along. We are so triggered by words, inference, images, and what we believe to be thinly veiled comments that we either retreat and go silent or go into full fight mode. Either action costs us our power to effect long-term systemic change This requires us to start with **Belonging Rule #1: *Turn into the Power***. Enacting this rule requires the grit, gumption, and gall to go against a direction that others are forcing you to take.

How we turn into the power is fundamental to success. We cannot accomplish this by using a battering ram or Trojan horse, assaulting with pure force to impose change. It is not shouting loudest or actively working to deconstruct or dismantle existing structures. It is not a binary right versus wrong—even when it is. Neither is it a call for raw, unfiltered activism. It is a recognition that circumstances have shaken our conscience and created an urgent need for people to return to the table, both to listen and understand a different point of view.

By turning into the power, we commit not to an extreme but to understanding, addressing, and using the power to individual and collective advantage. This requires strategic patience, an acceptance that incremental work is required. It demands that we get our hands dirty and wade into a pool of discomfort as we wrestle with the resistance—albeit necessary and healthy—that is sure to accompany any measure of change and the inherent conflict it creates.

By facing what is uncomfortable, we claim our own power. Only then can we begin to understand it. It allows us to steady and prepare ourselves—not for a fight, but for the tension that will surely follow. The tension this creates and the tension you feel is not just real but healthy. It is what connects us as humans, to each other and to our greater society. It is also necessary in our companies. Tension in an organization is a powerful force for good, especially when tethered to its existing power base.

For belonging to exist, we must recognize that there are inherent structures, intentional and unintentional, that either inhibit or encourage our ability to launch and sustain change. Too many people go for the quick, visible fix, rather than the long pathway to sustainable change. Yet, most people are open to such change; the challenge lies with its intensity and velocity.

Without turning into the power, we are relegating ourselves to being outsiders—the antithesis of belonging. Instead, seeking belonging affords us room to ask the most basic, often overlooked, questions: "What about this perspective, this idea, this thought, this possibility?" When we turn into the power, we are not saying, "I am right and you are wrong"; we are opening a space where diverse opinions can be heard and respected. We are finding a common ground to start challenging conversations. It allows us to state our truth, share our perspective, and be part of the conversation.

BELONGING AND POWER

In belonging, there is room for everyone. That means the solutions we are driven to adopt or implement must be for everyone. We cannot be inclusive for the few or just the existing power base. Inclusivity means including all. Yes, it's hard, but I assure you that you are up to the task. And that is at the heart of our explorations and challenges throughout this chapter and book. We will challenge the power structures that are assumed and those that are accepted solutions. DEI is not exempt from this examination, as we will challenge its individual and collective power as well as its role in the rules of belonging.

Belonging requires attention to be given to the whole. Effective, sustainable efforts must not answer to extremes on either side. Transformative momentum must engage the "moveable middle"—both the middle in our society and in our companies. Those in the middle thirst for information and understanding. If an effort stays on the fringe or is pushed to polarization, it can be enforced—but rarely adopted. Because the effort will not become a way of being, it will never make the organization or individual leader whole. This issue is tantamount to success in today's business and political environment. Leaders want to evolve and grow with our society, but the far reaches of the extremes distract and dissuade us from the real conversation and understanding required to create community and foster an environment where belonging can emerge and thrive. It is from this vantage point that we begin our efforts to turn into the power.

I will challenge you to think deeply, to feel uncomfortable exploring topics most try to avoid. Power is uncomfortable to take in or to think about, unless it is yours and you have little chance of losing it. That aside, power and the dynamics it creates in companies, departments, families, and communities are a necessary construct we must do more to understand, discuss, address, engage, and finally, where appropriate, turn into before we can begin to affect sustainable change. The walls cannot be torn down simply because we say, "Tear them down"; power will reconstruct and reinforce them without considering any other point of view.

Belonging demands difficult reflection followed by necessary actions. Belonging begins right here with how and where we tune in, turn in, and take action.

WHERE UNDERSTANDING STARTS—AND WHERE IT ENDS

As we move toward new understanding, we may still acknowledge what we've learned from the past. We must constantly remember, though, that it isn't only an ideology, a tradition, or a deeply rooted opinion that must change. Powerful structures are erected to support and protect investments of time, energy, and money that serve someone or something—sometimes simply to protect a leader. Whatever structure is in place, you can bet it isn't going to fall easily or simply morph to adopt new ideas, no matter how innovative the change or how obvious the need for it might be. In fact, when faced with a tsunami of change, incumbent power structures brace and rally forces to withstand a wave that carries something they don't want. The more entrenched the power base, the more likely it will prevail. The people in this base might make some superficial change—trying a new initiative, hiring a seemingly key employee, or making other adjustments that mimic compliance. The structure looks better but ultimately has gained little depth or value.

As leaders navigate and manage existing structures and power bases, their twists and turns, amplified by dedicated interests, may cause these leaders to undertake less-than-authentic responses and solutions. Amid an electrified ecosphere where everyone is reacting at once, leaders are juggling the demands of corporate boards, political whims, news cycles, and policies du jour. Too often, they just try to stay afloat long enough to create some breathing room. They end up responding to their constituencies with the safest solutions—the lowest common denominator, to avoid leaning too far in one direction. This carries the risk of losing support and often heralds a disastrous outcome. Leaders must understand that no one solution will please everyone; they must therefore act to force their way through the chaos, or risk being crushed under the weight of the opinions, needs, and expectations others set for them.

When leading, you must pause and recalibrate to determine not only what is right and the best way forward for your organization, but also what is right and the best way forward for intentional, positive, sustainable change. Leaders who accept short-term change for the sake of change and temporary appeasement must instead challenge themselves to strive for and accept systemic, long-term change—the only kind they should pursue. Short-term change is a waste that raises hopes and understandably creates greater disenfranchisement and disappointment long-term.

Although most of us understand power as the force that moves something in a direction, we often overlook the less-than-obvious ways in which existing organizational power structures are layered. They are complex and not always easy to identify. Rarely based on one thing, they are typically erected as a sort of scaffolding (as I explain in the next section). They may manifest as, for instance, the traditional white power structure, but more often are hidden behind different names and constructs. Leaders must take a holistic look at these structures to expose their interests and determine what actions will add real value, what will simply distract, and what will continue serving a status quo deeply entrenched in outdated agendas. The quick fix is appealing because it can relieve the immediate pressure, but it almost never leads to lasting or meaningful reform.

THE NATURE OF POWER

As noted, power exists as a force, a fluid energy that moves things in a direction. Power structures within organizations are erected over time and manifest as systems and incentives that encourage one thing at the expense of another. Never intended to endure as permanent arrangements, they become reinforced by practice or policy until they emerge as forces within the organization.

Power is most often created to serve the leader as well as one or more of three objectives, each of which I shall explain:

1. Money and resources
2. Velocity
3. Tradition, legacy, and status quo

Money and Resources: These amenities offer access, flexibility, comfort, and the ability to impose your desires and demands on others, where you can fall into a trap to win favor, priority, or status. They can provide stability but encourage risk taking. The dangerous part of money and resources is that the real risk often is imposed somewhere downstream of the money, when those dependent on this flow can become risk averse and feel pressured to conform.

Velocity: Force is being applied too hastily throughout today's society, without the necessary thought, knowledge, understanding, investigation, or consideration. Social media, societal polarity, bias, and lack of full disclosure or truth on the part of those who shout loudest, have the most followers, or best feed the agendas of influencers—all these phenomena fuel hasty calls for action to support or celebrate any proposed idea or opinion.

Tradition, Legacy, and Status Quo: These describe the ideas and actions that are so deeply rooted in us and in society, where structures have long been in place to keep things running smoothly, without challenge, because it is accepted as the way things work (or we are told they are best left alone). So many taboos and warnings have been built around these stalwarts that caution flags fly when anyone dares to challenge them.

Once these objectives gain support, over time a type of scaffolding begins to contain and promote them. Having observed these structures throughout businesses of all sizes and purposes, I group them under four categories: Leadership, Functions, Programs and Outcomes, and People. Alone, each can influence direction and change outcomes. They can blunt the force of an attack or serve as an impetus for change. Regardless, they are forces that must be accepted and understood individually as well as through the relationships and exponential power they create together.

Leadership: This structural group includes managers, executives, CEOs, boards of directors, and shareholders. Although each role has specific objectives, responsibilities, and input, together this full team can become an immutable component of how things operate. When their individual and combined power is effectively directed, things get done, teams work well together, and belonging has potential, if not viability. If there is ineptitude or there is complete resistance to change, then belonging will not flourish, much less be created. By contrast, management that overuses this structural level can seem heavy handed and stifle innovation and participation. In both extremes, there is little invitation or acceptance in participation of anything other than the approved or validated actions and attitudes.

Functions: This grouping of power structures includes human resources/performance management; the culture and tradition of the organization; and its communications and outward-facing efforts through social media, branding, and positioning. Again, each is necessary and fundamental to the organization's operation and healthy interactions. On the surface, these functions appear to establish, nurture, and sustain belonging. In reality, this is where belonging often stalls, owing to the unintended outcomes of policies, communications practices, and performance initiatives.

Programs and Outcomes: Here we find DEI programs, policies and procedures, health and safety initiatives, and a focus on finances and the bottom line. Talk about a structure loaded with potential pitfalls! This is where the basic expectations of the organization reside, along with the programs that set it up for success. When operated unchecked, however, any of them can become unwieldy and begin to overwhelm an organization, forcing it to abandon its purpose and inhibiting its progress.

People: Included here are external influencers such as customers, donors, fans, public opinion, and any other outside source providing input that informs direction, product development, or reputational or branding identities. This group also includes internal influencers: people with recognized authority or expertise, employee resource groups, unions, and other bodies of collective opinion. People feel the impact of power and can aid or impair its direction and impact. When their influence is imbalanced, people can overwhelm even the highest-functioning organizations and shift them onto unrecognizable paths.

The Powers in Play Are Often Not Obvious

Sometimes, when we are in a situation, we don't think about or clearly understand the structures that are encouraging or inhibiting our actions. Daily we are in the moment and take at face value what looks to be the most obvious. This is how the status quo moves along. Not until we become more deeply involved in an experience do the actual layers of power at play become recognizable, understood, or exposed.

This was true for me early in my career, when I was hired and enthusiastically brought on to a team because of what I thought was my talent, unique work experiences, and creativity. These were some of the traits that separated me from the other thousands of applicants who responded to the 1990s-era ad in the *New York Times*. I interviewed and completed a six-hour battery of writing assignments and thinking challenges before I was eventually hired to become an account executive in the sports marketing division of a top company in Boston.

I must admit that I was so thrilled to have been chosen that I didn't ask questions. I knew what the company did as well as its incredible reputation. I had no idea about its composition or any diversity efforts it had made. I just knew I was wanted and had earned a new job. I belonged. At least, I thought I did.

On my second day, the president of the company asked me to join her at a meeting at Reebok. To me, this was a dream come true: to be able to work with the giants in the sports industry of that time.

As we drove to the meeting, she asked if I knew why she had invited me to join her. I smiled and said, "Yes, I know sports as well as anyone."

She placed her hand halfway up my thigh and with a gentle squeeze, said, "No! They don't want to work with all women. I need a man at the table, so look smart and keep your mouth shut."

All I could think was, *Wow, what an opportunity*—not fully understanding that I was then the first and only man at the then forty-plus-person firm. I ended up taking the lead on the project, not because of my gender but because of my determination to make the project a success. Ironically, the project ended with the client firing us shortly thereafter, but my place at the firm was cemented.

As I reflect over my decades of work and life, it is interesting to think about the many power structures in this situation. The bold, visionary female president. The all-female company. The sports giant that wanted at least some male representation. They needed me as a man—and I suppose I needed them for my career progression.

What I realize is that through my work and accomplishments at the firm, I was accepted for who I was—not for what I was. I appreciated the unique position of being the token man. I didn't wallow in the fact that in every staff meeting, the employees were reminded that the company was established "for women, by women, for women's advancement." I embraced it. I could have felt minimized; I still only saw opportunity in being part of what I believed (and still do today) was one of the most innovative companies anywhere—with an extraordinarily visionary, future-oriented leader.

In chapter six, I'll introduce you to the concept of the belonging leadership tether, which explores your lifetime of experiences, situations, and environments in which you've developed your leadership style and grown to recognize not only how you have belonged but also how to create belonging for others. This job is marked on my tether because it taught me the life-changing lesson that *everything looks different from the outside*. At first, I quietly accepted my role and place in the company, not wanting to rock the boat. But, in time, I recognized that my value was being minimized by my unwillingness to speak up and share my unique views of the company and our work. The perceptions of an all-female company, the biases of a sports giant, and the idea that a token man had the power to change the dialogue were each put forward and challenged. As a man looking into the company, I grew to have a better appreciation for the uniqueness and the female focus of the firm. They, too, grew to appreciate the outsider's perspective—both from a man and, perhaps harder to appreciate, a Southern man. I appreciated what it was to be the only one of my kind, too, as well as the challenges it created for me and others around me, some of whom were not happy with my presence in the company.

But I didn't internalize any of those objections and projections. Leadership made a choice to hire me. My choice was to find a way to belong and fit into their well-established company. I didn't need to do anything different; I already *was* different, and my presence was the signal for change. And although the power base didn't change—yes, one or two men were added during my time—what did change was my ability to turn into that power structure and provide measurable value.

Symbols as Power Structures

The idea of belonging conjures many symbols. Signs, graffiti, well-placed words, and other aspects around us all evoke and deliver a message of belonging—whether we are included or excluded. These seemingly innocent symbols that we interface with daily actually serve as power structures on their own. Think about how DO NOT ENTER signs, MEMBERS ONLY posters, and red velvet ropes for VIPs each deliver a message. They serve as barriers, letting us know whether we belong, whether we are invited, whether we fit. These are more than social cues; they become directives that discourage us from trespassing or crossing barriers. Depending on our life experiences, we interpret the messages in various ways; some of us remain undeterred whereas others are frightened.

In our Leadership Learning Labs, we work on two particular symbols of belonging. The first is railroad tracks. These are a symbol of division. People talk about railroad tracks as if there is a good side and a bad side, the latter often a socioeconomically challenged area. "The wrong side of the tracks" evokes a strong response. Just the form of train tracks becomes a powerful structure in the community, even if it is a necessary structure for transportation.

The other structure is the white picket fence. We have such a fence in every Institute and Leadership Learning Lab. It serves as one of the most powerful reminders of the barriers and institutions that keep us in and others out—or vice versa. To some, it symbolizes the American Dream. Surrounding a pristine house, it has a majesty and simplicity. It is home. For too many others, the white picket fence conjures no identification at all. It is not part of their life experience; rather, it is the antithesis of the American Dream, a barrier within which they are never invited and they rarely fit in.

Regardless of the experience, we have all been in situations where we have been left out or have left other people out. We have been the recipient of the coveted invitation or the one left waiting for it, never to come. We have experienced knowingly and unknowingly what it feels like to be included and not to be included. The more that leaders are aware of their power to invite people in, the more effective they become. They need to understand that it is not about removing existing barriers but about clever ways to work with them and make them work for you. The picket fence must become a power statement of how you understand and creatively approach the very structures that mean to exclude you and others. No one has the right to keep you out—no matter the power structures in play.

THE LETTERS THAT BECAME BELONGING

There is no question that power structures within organizations, and those used by boards, include "lettered" initiatives and mandates, including DEI, ESG, and others. Leaders often advance them as the initiatives of the moment—and work to address them in whatever ways they can, either through a compliant or committed application within the company.

Regardless of how organizations attempt to implement them, these initiatives can create belonging and cause displacement at the same time. Depending on numerous factors, people conceive and adopt a logic around the programs' place and fit within the organization. Some initiatives intended to provide access and opportunity often rely too

FENCES THE OTHER SIDE

These reflection questions will help you contemplate and analyze feelings of belonging.

1. When was a time you felt outside of "the fence" or not a part of a group and someone brought you "inside"?

_____

2. How did that act of inclusion make you feel?

_____

3. How do you think that act of inclusion made the person who brought you "inside" feel? Do you think they struggled with that decision? Did they have anything to lose?

_____

4. Have you ever made an effort to include someone who may not have "fit in" to an environment that was comfortable for you?

_____

5. What did it feel like to be inclusive toward someone else?

_____

6. When was a time that you felt excluded because of something you couldn't control?

_____

7. How did that exclusion make you feel?

_____

8. Identify an instance in which you excluded someone.

_____

9. Was that exclusion intentional?

_____

10. Have you ever excluded someone for reasons they couldn't control?

_____

11. How do you think your active role in someone else's exclusion made them feel?

_____

12. If you could go back and act differently, would you?

_____

13. Have you ever reflected on that experience since?

_____

heavily on compliance over regard for longer-term change—which most of these programs are attempting to support, even if not in the stated or originally intended way.

Many initiatives that have led to today's understanding of belonging were often misunderstood from the very beginning, as leaders simply announced what they were going to do, instead of explaining why they were doing it and what they hoped to accomplish. Today, the "why" is too often hijacked by political extremes, making the origin story muddied, inconsistent, and misunderstood. This is true in society as well as in our own companies—and in families, too. Leaders have given too little context for the initiatives' importance, how they will serve the organization as a whole, and ultimately how they have performed, even as they may have increased marginalized employees' sense of belonging. When leaders realize that they can leverage these initiatives for financial gain and, more importantly, to increase any number of critical factors that support employee happiness and retention, they will begin to find more effective ways to not only implement them but also to nurture them more effectively within their companies' stated culture.

The challenge is when these programs become mandates and must-dos, or when political views are inserted into corporate initiatives that have nothing to do with politics. They do not last. Neither does the leader. Weaving them into the cultural fabric that is the company's DNA makes them more authentically accepted and experienced. But the crucial first step is that they must be understood to serve everyone, not just any one group.

Many of these initiatives have a deep historical perspective that the modern workforce either is unaware of, unsure of, or simply does not care about. Yet, understanding that many of today's DEI or ESG efforts, while more evolved, are connected to prior historical iterations of an attempt to make progress, especially in areas of DEI or DEIAB (diversity, equity, inclusion, accessibility, and belonging).

It is easy to assume that DEI is a relatively new concept, but the letters and the concepts have been represented for decades in many critical and visible initiatives. Most of what we are working through has familial roots in earlier programs and concepts, with a modern twist that addresses the needs of today.

We can look at concepts current and past and see how they are misunderstood, misused, or simply missing the mark for today's needs. Regulations and beliefs such as political correctness, affirmative action, Title IX, and cancel culture are each steeped in history, with origins going back anywhere from four decades to more than a century. In other words, they may be an active part of today's vernacular, effort, and even frustration, but they are not new—even if concepts around how organizations approach them can be presented as such.

Each of these directives, phrases, words, and efforts was well intentioned, helpful, insightful, and sometimes necessary, but over time people's energy for following them has become stale and rote—or, if lacking support and enthusiasm, forced and mandated.

To add a current perspective, let's consider the predecessors and precedents to many of the initiatives of today, whose roots are rarely discussed and often misunderstood. Each of the following concepts was an attempt to make inroads into and address systemic power struggles of their day. They were innovative and purposeful when they debuted, but they may have outlived their usefulness, no longer serving the complexities that organizations and individuals face in today's different world.

Political Correctness

This term refers to our use of language with the intentions of avoiding offending others, particularly when describing demographically diverse and traditionally marginalized groups (people with historically disadvantaged racial, gender, physical, or mental characteristics, or stigmatized cultural or sexual identities).

The history of the term is fascinating, originating in the Marxist–Leninist vocabulary that emerged following the Russian Revolution in 1917. Back then, being politically correct meant you abided by the doctrine of the Communist Party within the Soviet Union—the ultimate in compliance, where you went with the party line or else. Liberals and conservatives in the United States have volleyed this term between them, co-opting it in their chosen usage for decades.

In the workplace, political correctness has led to important equity shifts and inclusive norms; however, overreliance on political correctness also leads to failures in expressing 100% of the truth. People feel inhibited, afraid to address issues head-on or nervous about communicating a problem at all, and instead draw their own conclusions without questioning one another. These conclusions can burrow in, leading to resentment, avoidance, and declining performance. Companies are paying a price for the lack of authentic and often necessary dialogue—and so are their shareholders.

I have included political correctness as one of the great masqueraders, mainly because it is based on falsely making people comfortable. We've all been led in this dance and carefully taught the steps of acceptable behavior and tolerant language to such a point that it defers the uncomfortable conversations, often involving a flash point that adds the volatility of built-up resentment and deep hurt. According to a 2006 *Harvard Business Review* article, political correctness is a "double-edged sword," one that has enabled many historically disadvantaged group members to navigate their workplace environments with greater ease and more favorable perceptions of inclusion, but that has also reduced the capability of employees—including leaders—to build meaningful relationships that span potentially divisive group differences.

Affirmative Action

Affirmative action was enacted during President Lyndon Johnson's administration as a strategy to grant access to and expand opportunities for African Americans. Federal affirmative action policies debuted with the Civil Rights Act of 1964 and an executive order in 1965. The government forbade organizations receiving federal funding from using selection criteria that excluded or discriminated against African Americans.

Eventually, affirmative action was expanded to include women, Native Americans, Hispanic people, and other minority groups. It also broadened beyond private companies, including universities as well as state and federal government agencies. Since the 1970s and 1980s, the Supreme Court has gone back and forth on decisions regarding race-based affirmative action. The debate over whether to retain these policies continues today.

Harvard argues that more than 40% of universities rely on race as a factor in their admissions processes, and they have not found a race-neutral way to increase diversity in their student bodies. The question of how to foster diversity on college campuses without affirmative action in place is nuanced and challenging, but it is the heart of the debate. Doing so would require universities to publicly and continuously reinforce their commitment to diversity by developing and testing the effectiveness of race-neutral procedures that would effectively address the structural inequities that affirmative action was intended to fix.

Title IX

President Nixon's enactment of Title IX in 1972 was an early attempt at DEI, prohibiting any educational institution receiving federal funding from discriminating "on the basis of sex." The effects for women's access to educational opportunity were immediate and positive. To put this into context, in the early 1970s, 43% of college students were female, and men earned eight times the number of PhDs as women. Those numbers have now flipped, with women comprising the majority of college students and doctorate recipients. These patterns extend to physicians, dentists, and lawyers—women are achieving greater parity across the spectrum of industries.

Although great strides have been made in the arenas of education and athletics, the evolution of Title IX has also been polarizing and highly criticized by both conservatives and liberals. Democrats and Republicans have gone back and forth on policy, with President Obama's Department of Education issuing guidance to extend Title IX to sexual harassment policies and transgender students, and President Trump reversing such policies.

The issue at hand here is the evolution, the change of the law, to extend outside of the area of education and to shift to athletics, then beyond. The historic impact of Title IX is undeniable, but the question remains: Is it relevant and necessary for the world in which we live today, with companies and their leaders enforcing balance, diversity, and equity in the workplace? Title IX is at the greatest peril with the changing rules in athletics, in which colleges and universities are being forced to cut revenue-generating sports to fund other sports that are not financially sustainable. It is difficult to create an equitable university sports program when the football division, which drives the revenue for many athletic departments, must equalize the number of the scholarships it provides (eighty-five maximum) to its football players (men) while opening scholarships in other sports for the same number of women. Although there may be demand by the student athlete, the funding mechanisms—namely, demand from outside influences such as fans, television audiences, and donor bases—may not be enough to keep the sport alive. Universities must then consider how to drive funding and opportunities to women's sports in order to address this equity issue from its root causes. Future collegiate models may very well dictate the future of this historically important legislation.

Cancel Culture

The term "cancel culture" arguably originated as a 1980s slang term in black communities as a reference to breaking up with someone. Since then, the term has evolved substantially and today is applied in broad terms to show the velocity with which someone or something can fall out of favor. Canceled public figures can suffer reputational damage, lose their job or income, or be bullied relentlessly online and by members of the media who want to make a point or accelerate a provocative agenda. People continue to debate usage of the term, arguing about what it really means and how we should hold people accountable for past transgressions and present comments and actions taken out of context without becoming extreme.

In 2020, scientists at Pew Research polled Americans about their viewpoints on the term, including what it means and how they feel about it. The survey results were split, particularly along political lines. They found that 58% of US adults believe calling people out publicly on social media is more likely to hold them accountable, whereas 38% say it is more likely to punish those who don't deserve it. Democrats have a greater likelihood of believing that calling people out on social media for sharing offensive content is a way to hold them accountable (75% of Democrats vs. 39% of Republicans). Fifty-six percent of Republicans think "canceling" generally punishes people who don't deserve it, compared to 22% of Democrats.

When Pew Research coded the data further to explore patterns among the results, they found that about 17% of participants who believed that calling people out on social media holds them accountable regard it as a teaching moment that supports people's ability to learn from their mistakes and do better in the future. For respondents who say calling out others is an unfair punishment, a similar percentage (18%) believe it's because viewers can miss the context of a person's social media post or lack knowledge about the poster's intentions before confronting them.

The friction surrounding this set of actions can be ferocious, resulting in hasty judgment and punishment, and sparking discussion over whether canceling someone can authentically stem from a desire to hold others accountable. Because of the highly politicized world in which we live, I believe cancel culture has too often morphed into a weapon for the extremes. It inhibits psychological safety and impedes important and necessary dialogue from a fear of labeling and erasure. It is often accompanied by a level of self-righteousness and as such cedes power to the loudest and often most judgmental voices. Taken to extremes, cancel culture can resemble a police state where nobody knows the rules, which enforcers morph to fit the changing needs of any individual or group on a whim. This anxiety creates a very challenging work dynamic that limits and even discourages the connectedness that companies need and their employees crave. Further, it helps to exacerbate the Great Disconnect, which is fueled by a lack of authenticity and the threat of being ostracized at work or, worse, at home or in the community.

DEI and Belonging

As we process today's imperatives, DEI is accepted as today's standard. It is revered. It is mandated. It is measured. And it can be effective. However, when considered in the structural composition of how organizations work and thrive, DEI is stifled by limited ability and insufficient effort.

At many companies, DEI policies, programs, personnel, and efforts are completely ineffective. They have become an internal wedge that divides the power bases, many of which are high performers. Instead of DEI's intended purpose of increasing diversity, equity, and inclusion, sometimes it does the opposite by pushing out the existing power base with little conversation about or regard for its historic value and continuing contributions.

As you will find throughout this book, once the momentum is pushed to the extremes, the middle shuts down and ceases effective participation in any given initiative or action. The disregard of DEI programs for the middle's voice comes from using it to meet an agenda, instead of understanding the middle and addressing diversity, equity, and inclusion as realistic, business-positive imperatives. Rather than pushing to extremes, efforts to bring people into the center of the discussion and the desired outcome is what begins to create belonging.

When a power base arises from a singular or limited issue, like DEI efforts, it rarely creates the preferable longer-term change and sustainable adoption. Unfortunately for the leader, velocity can take an issue too far, too fast, without effectively integrating or embedding it in the organization's culture. Leaders can only establish belonging when they engage the entire organization, which ensures that there is space for all—or at least all who want to be part of important ongoing societal evolution.

We see this often when DEI coordinators are hired or DEI committees created at historically white institutions. For example, Shawna Jackson was hired as chief diversity officer at a large state institution. Under tremendous scrutiny, she turned into the power; challenged the traditions and structures that had been constructed to constrain progress; and transformed her community with her vision, generosity, and leadership.

Shawna was hired because of her qualifications, organizational fit, and vision. The organization was working through various complex social and racial issues internally, in the community, and within its broader constituency. They invested significantly in community engagement outreach and wanted long-term systemic change—not the often popular, showy quick fix. This effort toward diversity was a core component of their strategic plan, and they worked hard to find the right person to meet their goals.

Despite her impeccable academic and work pedigree, Shawna faced immediate backlash from various organizational power structures, both for her gender (she was the first woman in this position following four successive male leaders) as well as her leadership style of approaching change in a less aggressive or confrontational manner. Her first ninety days were a brutal reminder of the harsh realities of fitting in a new environment—even for a respected leader. She was prepared for opposition from the traditional white male power base, but instead, found the black male power base to be more vocal and resistant to being led by a black woman.

Shawna's early days were dominated by behind-the-scenes gossip, personal questioning, and open attacks. Her distinguished and brave exterior encased a vulnerable, thoughtful leader—two vital characteristics for which she was hired. Through her unflappable commitment to lasting change through a clear vision, a defined plan, and financial support, she has made significant headway by dismantling existing power structures in a steady manner. Still, the bruising fights at the start of her tenure from people she thought would be allies left her questioning what new structures needed to be established to support continued, meaningful progress.

Shawna defined her leadership as one of broader inclusion, not simply activism, as was the style of her predecessors. She established herself as leading in order to effect change, not to be known as the loudest or most aggressive voice. Activism was a well-worn effort in the position she now occupied, one that had had limited progress. By contrast, her preferred approach was to build a wider base and invite people in. This approach was better aligned with the organization's vision of leadership and paved the way for powerful groups to become more engaged, ultimately fulfilling her intention to expand the department's power base.

By inviting people in, Shawna worked to engage the moveable middle, even with extremists noisily demanding attention for their dissenting point of view. She realized that the only way forward was not to concede her beliefs or doubt her place in the process, but instead to go directly into the historic power base—surprisingly, not the power base she anticipated—rather than the activist power base.

Shawna won over the middle by building a platform to serve the disenfranchised as well as everyone in the organization. It immediately changed the external perception of her function. She openly laid out what her department believed and did not believe was their responsibility. She shared her past and present passion for this work. Then she presented an initial approach to how she would develop the strategy and craft an intentional culture for the department. Shawna asked for every voice to be counted and heard through interviews, surveys, and assessments of people's hopes and dreams for the department.

The results were powerful. The survey scores and interviews demonstrated a palpable divide between long-term middle managers and Shawna's new leadership. She was undeterred. She worked to create a space where people were invited to talk, listen, adopt new understandings, and be part of a new vision. She was able to use their information and differences to convert them to accept her vision. They chose to trust and follow her. Shawna's message was that belonging includes everyone and that this should be evident in every aspect of the organization. People were invited in who had never previously been asked to share their perspective or to join in creating a new reality that would include all. Shawna brought power and voice to people previously pushed out of the conversation. As a result, she has transformed her organization and community with her vision, generosity, and leadership. She turned into the power and transformed it to something that could be redistributed to her people.

UNINTENDED CONSEQUENCES

I hear stories daily from leaders who care deeply about doing right but struggle to live up to the goals set by those to whom they report, including their boards. Do they take shortcuts and create a window-dressing solution for the quick fix, or do they take a hit to their own stated performance criteria by working toward the longer-term solution? It is an ongoing dilemma that reveals the incongruity between what leaders are asked to do and what they are tasked to do. They are often asked to solve a problem more systemically, but their incentive packages coerce them to go for the swifter, more visible fix. I find great conflict in the pull to promote a quick fix that will appease the extremes and the loudest voices. And I often see how committed leaders want to address the root of the issues but feel strong pressure to quiet the chaos.

Take the leader of a hiring committee. He and his diversely composed committee were tasked with reviewing who should be recommended for partner at the firm. They undertook a thorough review based on preestablished and rigorous data-driven metrics and performance criteria—the same for each person. Four candidates met the scrutiny of the defined metrics and were recommended by the hiring committee. Yet, the CEO, whose bonus structure and that of his leadership team depended on diversity gains, directed the head of the committee to change the scoring and elevate one of the women not selected in the original recommendations to be among the top four candidates.

The committee leader replied that the woman not only was not in the top seven of the eight candidates based on the data and her prior performance; she also had a series of documented behavioral issues the past year that were inconsistent with the company's stated policies. The CEO responded, "Add her, period." The selected candidate didn't earn this hire—it was given, at a cost to her, her future employees, and the committee who knew better. It did the opposite of creating belonging; it started a division within the inner ranks of the company, including the employees whom she had previously managed. But, in the end, the CEO got his bonus for promoting diversity.

Unfortunately, he pushed for this hire without examining the systems in place that would create a baseline culture of belonging. It's not about promoting the one; it's about figuring out how to uplift the many. The board and the CEO put structures in place for themselves (like the diversity accountability metric) but not for the people they intended to support. Instead, they should have asked themselves the following questions:

- Why does this group lack diversity in the first place?
- How can we ensure that women and racial/ethnic minorities in our organization are getting the right opportunities to ensure they can ascend into leadership positions?
- Who are we attracting, and how can we expand our pool of candidates in the future?

The outcome focus is better served when all elements of the attraction–selection–attrition pipeline address the systemic issues and shared biases that prevent qualified diverse candidates from being considered for and ascending to leadership roles.

Organizations contain many power structures. Some are helpful, but many produce unintended consequences. These can be as innocuous as the wrong hiring process or a performance system that fails to provide honest, sometimes uncomfortable feedback. Research shows that lack of such feedback is a growing concern for female and minority employees: without it, they remain at a disadvantage versus those receiving more direct feedback. Other power structures include a culture that does not embrace belonging. And some of the easier-to-fix structures include the misaligned incentives that plague not only the leader but also leadership across the organization. Without alignment on what really matters, midlevel managers and employees may perpetuate the status quo by keeping in place what they have experienced and what has historically worked for them. As leaders, we must become more aware that the difference is the exceptions that are made. Exceptions become long-term power structures themselves that will eat away at the performance framework if left unaddressed.

The power structure that is DEI will remain at the forefront of organizational initiatives and efforts for decades. The question is, how can leaders depoliticize these efforts and implement them more effectively? Simple: by turning into the power mindset. Leaders must challenge the current status quo by first separating and then recalibrating the sequencing and placement of belonging in the diversity, equity, and inclusion ecosystem. Each aspect of DEI has its own importance. Yet, when organizations aggregate all three, they risk diminishing the importance of each and taking less-targeted pathways to accomplish them—especially when the performance metrics are geared to measuring the mingled whole. It may be a nuance, but it is an important one. Better to move belonging to the front of the conversation and the leader's expectations. Belonging envelops the entirety of the desired outcome, of which diversity, equity, and inclusion are parts. For an organization to achieve its people-focused goals, belonging must be perched atop as a depoliticized framework that builds commonality, unity, and community.

We cannot belong or create belonging for others if we are unwilling to do what is uncomfortable by turning into the power. That turn, that willingness to face obstacles in our direct path, that confidence to speak up, that courage to ask the real question, that ability to recognize the necessity of challenge, and the readiness to do it—this is the power that belongs to each of us. This is where our commitment to belonging begins: not by ignoring or circumventing power but by turning directly into it.

POWER BALANCE

Mapping Power Structure

Plot each power structure on the line below, evaluating the extent to which you feel the structure is being wielded ineffectively (e.g., there is an underuse of the power structure or level of ineptitude, creating negative outcomes), effectively (e.g., there is a healthy and balanced use of the power structure, creating positive and effective outcomes), or excessively (e.g., there is an overuse or overreliance on the power structure, creating negative outcomes).

POWER	0	1	2	3	4	5	6	7	8	9	10
LEADERSHIP											
Board of Directors/Shareholders											
CEO											
Executive Leadership											
Managers											
FUNCTIONS											
HR/Performance Management											
Legal											
Culture and Traditions											
Communications/Social											
PROGRAMS/OUTCOMES											
Financial/Bottom Line Focus											
Policies and Procedures											
Health and Safety Initiatives											
DEI Programs											
PEOPLE											
External Influencers *(customers, donors, fans, followers, public opinion, etc.)*											
Internal Influencers *(groups, long-term employees, employee resource groups, unions, etc.)*											
	INEFFECTIVE-USE ZONE				EFFECTIVE-USE ZONE				EXCESSIVE-USE ZONE		

REFLECTION:

1. Which power structures would you diagnose as being in the "effective-use" zone? What makes them operate in a balanced, effective, and healthy state, one that improves outcomes and enhances belonging?

   _____

2. How might you leverage the structures in the middle—the ones you've diagnosed as healthy and effective—to pull on the structures that are being ineffectively used or excessively relied upon?

   _____

3. What power do you have in your organization? Which structures can you exert influence on in a positive way? How can you raise awareness about existing power imbalances (e.g., ineffective use, excessive use)? Which power structure(s) raise the greatest concerns in your organization?

   _____

4. What are the first three steps you could take to pave the way for positive change? Who is your first point of contact? What additional resources or support do you need? How will you make your case?

   _____

Chapter 2

,WHO IS WHITE,

Belonging Rule #2: **LISTEN WITHOUT LABELS**

L abeling is part of life, both our thinking and everyday speech, yet unfortunately we use it to include or exclude people and important concepts. We put little thought into the words and labels we naturally choose—they are simply part of our way of communicating. Some labels—even those as simple as "white" or "black," "young" or "old," "wealthy" or "poor," "conservative" or "liberal"—may be accurate, but in context may be irrelevant or inappropriate. Labels can bring us inside or leave us outside. When we actively use labels to exclude people, we limit understanding. We take away who they really are and what they have to contribute. We disallow real and necessary conversations by diminishing or oversimplifying the worth of the people we label or, less often, by elevating their place. We also frequently use labels to telegraph our take on the world.

Labels are often an easy and convenient shorthand to put people or concepts in a certain bucket or category. The label changes the context and meaning—sometimes in degrees, but often in more destructive ways. And it comes at a cost. Take the over-simplified labels used to describe, and reduce, generations to their supposed "shared" attributes. It reduces all to their perceived lowest common denominator—which, coincidentally, is not shared by all members. It is a gross generalization that all within that generation are expected to be, to act, and to think alike. There is no group that is in full agreement or shares a homogeneous perspective on anything—not even within a family—regardless of how closely they are affiliated. By using a reductionist label, it makes it easy for the labeler, but comes with a cost related to how we listen, understand, accept, and ultimately act or respond.

Labels have always existed, but they are more prevalent today as we struggle to sort out the complexities of what we think we know and don't know. Labels can inflame any kind of conflict or controversy. During vitriol and volatility, there is a rush to label as we slice up what is at stake and who is a potential stakeholder. This rush is our means of protecting our ideas or ourselves and provides a measure of control—or at least perceived control—in challenging times. As our political environment has continued to evolve or devolve, depending on your perspective, labeling has become a dangerous and divisive force. The rush to label has harmed our ability to listen, communicate, and understand.

This brings us to **Belonging Rule #2: Listen Without Labels.** This rule requires us to hear what is actually spoken, without judgment, while engaging the unspoken with humanity and heart. In other words, it requires us to understand the whole of what is shared and limit our natural inclination to translate meaning by applying our own or someone else's labels.

REDUCED TO A LABEL

In 2020, several weeks after the murder of George Floyd, a group of student athletes at the University of Texas at Austin (UT) presented a list of demands to the university's interim president, Jay Hartzell, about perceived issues of racism and a lack of a sense of belonging for students of color. The demands were each considered, including a highly volatile and controversial demand to replace the century-plus-old university alma mater, "The Eyes of Texas," which students believed to be of racist origins and usage. The university responded by addressing many of the recommendations (including programming, financial support, and renaming of buildings), going further on its own initiative in many areas of increased focus and commitment.

However, when it came to replacing the alma mater, Hartzell had three choices: keep the song as is with no discussion; modify or replace the song; or the third and most difficult option, keep the song while commissioning a group to study its history, and encourage dialogue and learning around it. The university chose the third option: keeping the song while commissioning a group to study and report its full history. Due to the contentious nature of the issue and the intensity of the global dialogue, Hartzell laid out clear expectations for the research process. If something unexpected and egregious arose from the research, he was committed to eliminating or changing the song. However, he believed that as a research university, UT had an inherent duty and responsibility to use research to inform a deeper understanding and fuel ongoing dialogue, no matter how difficult or volatile. Preparing students to discuss challenging topics while remaining in community is fundamental to the university and its role in shaping the next generation of leaders.

What followed was an in-depth exploration that would culminate in a report on the full history and intention of the song. You could say that journey was the beginning of this book. It was a year that changed my life and perspective. Early in the process, I was asked my thoughts on the controversy. I shared my opinion with the university's leadership and then provided my professional approach to addressing and resolving the issue. I realized shortly after presenting that the only acceptable answer was to listen. President Hartzell strongly agreed and asked me to become his eyes and ears as he focused on and navigated many complex issues across the university related and unrelated to the song. So that's what I did.

One thing that was certain to me was the fact that there was so much hurt and such a deep desire to be heard. The process started with sixteen interviews, which then morphed into thirty-two, organically growing into more than thirty-five hundred conversations over seven months. I spoke to students, band members, athletes, alumni, leaders of alumni groups (including the largest black alumni group), faculty, coaches, and staff, as well as others who wanted to be heard. Perhaps the most life-changing interviews were those with members of the UT community known as Precursors, the first black members of the University dating back to 1956. I listened to their stories and tried to imagine what it was like to be them in a very different time, yet now facing many of the same social issues. My heart was ripped out as they described their raw and personal early experiences as students decades before. I was surprised to learn that even with their continuing questions of the past and UT's current decisions, they genuinely loved the university and took pride in its evolution.

Even more unexpected were the Precursors' stories of personal struggles with and evolving views on the alma mater and their personal ownership of it. I began to question my own experiences and potential sources of ignorance or bias—what else did I not know? What had I perceived incorrectly or made assumptions about? What about the history of our country, my state, my university? Had I been unaware, or had I simply ignored it because it didn't appear to be about me? It became not only a professional quest but a deeply personal one as well.

I had the honor of listening to people's perspectives and probing into their feelings and emotions. These open conversations gave them a place to be heard and, in some cases, to vent their anger, frustration, fears, and concerns about both the past and the future. My only promise was to take their stories and share them with the interim president and the committee formed to study "The Eyes of Texas." I promised to listen and only to respond if I was attacked or if the facts were misunderstood or misrepresented. The conversations filled my head and emptied my soul as interviewees displayed in words and emotion their deep hurt and feeling of not belonging. But I heard and shared their message.

Being part of the committee with Rich Reddick, at the time the associate dean for equity, community engagement, and outreach in UT's College of Education and now dean of undergraduate studies, was a life-changing experience. More than any title can express, this man is one of the most thoughtful, courageous, and brilliant scholars and humans with whom I have ever worked. We developed a bond that allowed us to talk about every challenging social issue in its most honest and raw form. No difference or characteristic separated us; we were unified in our goal to learn and understand history and its impact today.

We organized a comprehensive committee plan to bring people including renowned historians, academicians, students, and alumni, with wildly different beliefs and strongly held perspectives together for critical dialogue and understanding. We led this group with intensive weekly meetings: more than fourteen full committee meetings, as well as subcommittee meetings and countless small-group discussions—on Zoom and with some in person. We knew that we had to create trust, and we did. We ultimately produced a fifty-eight-page fact-based report, supported with reams of data and research as well as individual testimonials from committee members and outside experts. Anticipation of its findings was high.

Much to various people's disappointment, the report never labeled "The Eyes of Texas" as good or bad; it simply laid out its complete history for people to base their own judgment on the facts and their individual life experiences. The collective information was powerful and had the potential to be transformative. Our goal was not to change people's minds, but rather to give them information to process and facts to process on their own.

Many articles preceded the release of the official report, most filled with assumptions, misinformation, and mistruths. They were written to capitalize on the national narrative that had brought both media interest and scrutiny from across the country. Incorrect information was abundant, backed by naysayers, political operatives, and other opponents of the song, with the intent of biasing those most impacted. It was a perfect example of inside and outside influencers creating a negative groundswell, calling for the university to preempt the report and influence its possible decision to keep the song beyond the study period.

Within hours of the report's release, the first media story appeared online in a popular, widely read monthly magazine. The article was balanced, thoughtful, and well documented. But something stood out for me. I noticed that Rich Reddick, my partner and friend in this research effort, was qualified in the first line as follows: "Rich Reddick, who is black . . ." What I didn't fully understand, or really think about, was how my friend would react to that line. I called Rich to get his reaction to the article, and his disappointment and hurt—directly related to the mention—were clear. Yes, he was hurt by the black label, even though he is immensely proud of his heritage. But, it was not why he was chosen to lead this prestigious work—it was his qualifications, experiences, judgment, insights, and love for his university.

My immediate reaction was to acknowledge his hurt; to agree that, certainly, it was wrong; and to suggest that I call the publication to try to have those words removed. Rich said to leave it alone. He asked for nothing except understanding. But the words hit him so hard that I felt compelled to act. I immediately called the writer, who shared that it was never part of his original story submission—someone else at the magazine had inserted it. Ultimately, the publication decided to revise the story and remove any mention of Rich's race. They agreed that the color of someone's skin was not relevant to the story—even a story steeped in race.

As much as I heard about why it bothered Rich, I could never fully realize his pain. That is, not until a few months later, when an online story was published about me and my work at the University of Texas. The writer began her description of my role with "Brad Deutser, who is white . . ."—an echo of what Rich had experienced. Nothing else mattered in the story to me. The inaccuracies in reporting, the facts that were omitted, the misstatements—nothing. The reporter didn't care to understand that there were more than thirty-five hundred interviews, which I had conducted for one purpose: *to listen and understand*. I knew what had actually happened, and so did the thousands of people with whom I interacted throughout the process. Yet, all I could see in that article was the label—*Brad Deutser, who is white*.

It cut deep, much to the surprise of everyone who knew me. Most were baffled by my reaction, stating, "Well, you *are* white." But they missed the message. They didn't understand that the color of my skin was not what was defining to me in my work—it was my ability to listen with compassion and genuinely connect with people where they are and as who they are. I was able to be fully present in the moment with multiple Precursors recounting their experiences; to be with an African American band member struggling over how to commit to playing a song when she didn't fully understand its history; or to work hand in hand with the president of the African American alumni association, which was deeply divided over the issue. I was able to connect because of who I am—regardless of my race. Yet, I was reduced to simple skin color by a reporter more interested in clicks than journalistic integrity. She tried to belittle my being in the conversation with my work in diversity, equity, and inclusion. Imagine both stories without any mention of skin color, mine or Rich's. My color mattered—to the writer and to me, but in very different ways. In both Rich's and my case, our lives' work was reduced to one label. Our place in the conversation was called into question simply because of the color of our skin—not the skill set, knowledge base, or unique experience we brought.

In fact, those three words caused me to question not only my place in a field with complex social, political, and racial issues, but also my place alongside the many hundreds of people from different backgrounds and cultures with whom I had formed bonds and deep friendships through my work.

I felt vulnerable, and everywhere I went I began to believe that before I even said a word, the audience was applying "who is white" and filtering every subsequent word though this singular lens. This simple phrase is true at face value, yet what I imagined them really saying and thinking was, "You don't belong in this conversation." My closest colleagues challenged me to own the words and make it even more core to my work, my teachings, and my understanding of leadership. I began to talk more openly to other leaders—Black, Hispanic, Asian, White, LGBTQ+, Jewish, Muslim, Christian—about identity, understanding, and the labels others want to apply in order to reduce us to something easily grasped, without form or individuality. There will always be labels that work for some while hurting others. That is part of the destructive power of labels, even when a label such as "who is white" is accurate.

THE LINK BETWEEN LABELING AND BIAS

Labeling occurs when we use one word or phrase to represent a group of characteristics or qualities. Of course, that is one of the functions of language—to communicate constructs and concepts that can include generalized understanding. Recalling our conversation in chapter one about political correctness, however, it isn't just the choice of words that we're exploring here, but instead how the brain applies meaning to the words we're absorbing when we are processing information. This is fundamental to how we must challenge ourselves to Listen without Labels.

Much of our current instinct to block belonging comes from decades of layered bias accentuated by labeling. The human brain—specifically, an ancient part of it—is hardwired to label because it helps us simplify the world around us and more easily tell where threats lie. This part is constantly operating a risk assessment, which today can include inappropriately assessing difference by assigning people to neatly typified groups (e.g., "black" vs. "white" or "man" vs. "woman"). Labeling helps our brains deal with an overwhelming amount of informational input and stimuli. Unfortunately, our tendency to label also perpetuates stereotypes and, if left on autopilot, devoid of rational thought and executive function from the frontal lobe of the brain, impedes inclusion. Classic research has demonstrated that the words we use can determine how we view people—meaning that our labels, even when completely false, make us think and feel a certain way about others.

We know that labels, in containing subtle biases, tend to increase power differentials and fuel further inequity and exclusion. Yet, we don't yet know how to sufficiently address use of labels in the workplace. A recent study on workplace interventions targeting subtle organizational bias indicates that organizations are doing little to foster the interpersonal skills (e.g., apologizing or forgiveness) needed when people engage in biased behavior.

While it's important to become aware of our biases, research demonstrates that awareness doesn't always lead to behavior change. We need to understand how to talk about labels, communicate about bias, and move forward when transgressions occur. Too often, we are quick to fill in the gaps and respond for the sake of response. In fact, these situations require us to slow down, to listen and carefully process the pathway forward. Our instinct is to rapidly revert to our historic thought processes and closed-off ways of processing—but in these situations, speed is not our ally. Instead, we must shift the impulsive elevated response to thoughtful learning, evolution, and then, if warranted, behavioral change.

Labeling is pervasive in our thoughts and attitudes about what makes us "good" at something, who deserves a seat at any table, who is the right fit for a job or task, and even who is more "like" us. The ultimate purpose of labels is to apply a single word or phrase to what others will generally understand as a set of behaviors or characteristics.

Positive labels can open doors, expedite access, and speed acceptance. Negative labels create barriers, raise suspicion, and injure opinion. Labeling is so layered that you may have missed how we've just applied two labels: "positive" and "negative."

In my company's Leadership Learning Lab and Institute for Belonging, we use the white picket fence described in chapter one to help people see, reflect upon, and explain the problems with labeling. The white picket fence is a decades-long symbol. To some it represents the American Dream of a perfect life: a safe and comfortable house, a neatly trimmed lawn, and the opportunities that provide the physical elements of a happy life. To others it represents a barrier, welcoming those with all the privilege, gifts, talents, and advantage—all the right stuff—while blocking others from entry and participation. Of course, real physical structures of inclusion and exclusion are constructed with a variety of materials; sometimes they are symbolic, others metaphorical. But make no mistake that labeling exists to indicate acceptance or to justify questioning or even blocking your right to be somewhere.

Labels often show up in one of the following contexts:

- To serve as a boundary, in an act of dominance and control, to keep you out—or in
- To put you in a place of someone else's choosing, projecting qualities and characteristics on you that have nothing to do with your actual identity
- To one-up you, showing you and others that you don't belong at the table; often accomplished through ridicule or false superiority
- To help you understand a complex problem or situation by distilling it to its simplest form, almost always its lowest common denominator

BEHIND THE WORDS

There's been so much dislocation and change in our world that people are confused—and hurting. You don't necessarily know their pain, but you can likely guess at some of it. Are you responsible for relieving the pain of others? This is where every aspect of being human comes in. Their pain may not be your pain, but we all know what pain is. Their path may not be your path, but we are all travelers. We all, regardless of how we are labeled, have experienced being on the outside of a conversation, a relationship, an opportunity. And, in those moments, we know the hurt we felt.

When we approach people with respect and openness, we create a safe space where pain can be shared, heard, understood, and transformed. When we respect the unique experiences of another, it opens us to new perspectives and possibilities. In chapter one, we talked about turning into the power. Listening without labels is about tuning in to the pain—to what is said and what is unsaid—and avoiding unnecessarily filling in any blanks in someone else's story. Hearing how a string of words knits together gives insight to an experience or history that means something to the other person. People's feelings and experiences are as varied as their physical presentation. They are individualized. They can be predictive, triggering, inspiring, or enlightening. They can bring dysfunction, awareness, and sensitivity to something you've never imagined.

HOW TO LISTEN WITHOUT LABELS

We are all experts at listening. But we are not always attuned to hearing or being fully engaged with what someone is thinking, feeling, or actually trying to convey. It is important to pause and reflect on how actively you listen, and how quickly you have the urge to respond. We forget that we can listen without actually hearing the spoken word.

Sometimes, we listen by simply watching someone's expressions or feeling their energy. We can use our other senses to help us process and use our brain and its flight, fight, or freeze mechanism to slow our response. Some of the best and most empathetic listeners are those that actually practice this lost art. The following are some of the practices and approaches I use.

- **Start with the reason you are in the conversation.** Make sure your reason is understanding, growth, or learning. When you start with the goal of arguing and defending your point, you are not listening. If your purpose is to change someone, you are starting at a disadvantage. Instead, identify shared goals; listening and learning may be the paramount reason you are together in dialogue, but if there are other goals that can bridge differences, start there.
- **Understand the who.** The person is not an adversary—even if they are. They are a person. Allow them to be human . . . to be an individual.
- **Put a face on them.** If you don't know the person, you're early in the relationship, or not with them in person, it may be helpful to imagine that you are talking to a friend or family member. This is not intended to diminish the person's identity, but rather to change how open you are to listening to them. When we talk to those closest to us, we are more likely to give them the benefit of the doubt than we might a stranger.
- **Eliminate the "Why?"** The word "why" creates a gap that someone must cross, creating an adversarial conversation and placing people in opposition. "Why" pushes them back on their heels versus standing as equals. The question is important and so is how you frame it. Simply ask: "Tell me about . . . ," "Can you share . . . ," or "Help me understand . . ."
- **Ask questions to understand.** Don't question solely as a setup to countering with an attack or to belittle or minimize.

It is important to ask clarifying questions such as, "Can you tell me more about . . ." rather than assuming you disagree on every point. Questioning may reveal common ground.

- **Stay away from any guiding language** such as, "Don't you think that . . . ," "I'm sure you would agree . . . ," or "Yes, but . . ." Instead, after you have asked clarifying questions, close the discussion by paraphrasing. Summarize the key points you heard: for example, "I heard . . ." or "I am hearing you say . . ."

- **Actively listen.** Listen to the words they are saying, their facial expressions, and their body movements. Make eye contact and retain an open (rather than a defensive) posture. Relax your facial muscles. Also, be mindful of your tone of voice and ensure you are empathic and warm, rather than hostile or patronizing.

- **Show you are listening.** Sometimes it is appropriate to write down salient points and perspectives to show you are listening, especially if the conversation becomes contentious. Writing down their points can also help you to reduce unconscious biases, as it forces you to focus on what the other person is saying rather than mentally running your own script focused on your thoughts and perspective. You may also want to ask clarifying questions, probing a point you or the group need to unpack further. Other times, simply acknowledge you have heard by repeating what someone else has shared. Even if you disagree.

- **Defuse personal attacks.** One method is to say, "This is not about me or you, it is about us understanding the issue or our different perspectives. Let's stay focused on the facts and not attack each other." If disrespect continues, it may be best to stop the conversation in a respectful way. For instance, "Let's revisit this conversation at a later time. I need time to process my thoughts, and the more personal this becomes, the further away we get from actually hearing each other."

- **Go for the "aha!" not the win.** It's the understanding that counts. Be a student. Try to learn one thing new in every conversation. We are so accustomed to posturing for the win that we lose the opportunity to grow and evolve.
- **Don't be the judge and jury.** Listening is about gaining perspective and understanding. Acknowledge to yourself that you may have both conscious and unconscious biases that can serve as distractions, and try to put them aside. Combat the urge to judge by approaching with curiosity.
- **Avoid the conclusion.** It is not about rushing to an answer, it is about the conversation and both hearing and being heard. It is okay if there is no resolution and no conclusion. The act of listening and hearing is the value in the conversation.
- **Create closure through acknowledgment.** I try to end every conversation, even the most challenging and heated, with some form of positivity. Often I simply thank the other person for sharing and for giving me something new to consider. You do not have to validate their perspective, only be respectful in hearing what they have to say.
- **Take time to acknowledge and celebrate each other's willingness to have the conversation.** Thank the other person for being open and honest, for being willing to discuss things in the first place. Getting out of your echo chamber and seeking to learn from an opposing perspective fuels growth. That is the win.
- **Communicate availability to explore.** Not all conversations need to be long, but you do need to be fully present. Communicate a willingness to listen, and if time is limited, be sure to say, "If we need longer, we can get together again, no problem." Willingness is a key to establishing trust. In a busy world, you can show respect by responding with timeliness and then schedule more time later if there is more to be said. That way, your interest and commitment are evident. Sometimes,

we put off conversations because we don't have the time; this is why it is so important to let the other person know that you care enough to spend the appropriate time to listen, even if you don't have it in that moment.

The labels we apply can mistakenly convince us that we are on opposite sides of an issue, a value, a needed action, or a governing opinion. But approaching someone in opposition won't get you very far and is likely to reinforce any label already applied. Rich Reddick suggests that we acknowledge our difference of opinion with another and, along with that, start from a place of respecting those with whom you do not agree or understand. "We respect the fact that you've got a voice, you want your voice out in the world," he says, "and we understand or at least empathize with the fact that there are some terrible things happening in the world and that you want to respond to those things."

Rich also advises, "Start from the space of empathy and understanding. If you don't understand, endeavor to understand. What do I need to read? What do I need to be exposed to? What spaces do I need to be in so I can be a better empathizer in what's happening in this space?"

Rich reminds us that starting with empathy doesn't mean you have to be on the same page in everything. He proposes that you simply think about what it might feel like to be at that stage of your life, or in a situation where you might have had a similar thought or feeling. Imagine looking at the world that you see and feeling like you're not being heard, or not getting a chance to put your perspectives forward. When you act with empathy, you can more easily find the grace to consider another perspective.

You may feel you've reached a point where you are at an impasse on a given topic or situation. Even so, when we commit to responding with respect, listening without labeling, and applying empathy, we build an expectation that together, we both can work through something.

Rich continues, "When you enter a conversation with the idea that you can either defeat the other person's arguments or convince them to come to your side, it doesn't work. Most likely, you're going to end up in a space where you might find some places of agreement but you're going to probably end up in a place where you're like, 'No, I'm not quite on the same page as you are in this whole thing and that's okay. There is no absolute right or absolute wrong, but instead various chains of better to worse responses."

You cannot listen without labels if 100% agreement is your goal. Agreement may require multiple conversations, finding common ground by focusing on shared and similar values, and recognizing places where you can agree, in order to unpack the many factors that are influencing both or each of you. Stripping the conversation of applied labels opens the way for honest conversation.

WHAT WE LEARNED FROM "THE EYES OF TEXAS"

The "Eyes of Texas" debate started when UT student athletes presented a list of demands to the university. Logan Eggleston, a nationally top-ranked volleyball star and a person who has become a trusted colleague and dear friend, was one of the students who had helped compile the list.

Logan describes the origin of the demands as follows: "A group of athletes came together, and we also talked to students in different organizations asking, 'What are you guys asking for from the university?' and we all had this really positive conversation of things that we wanted to see so we worked together to make a list. We understood, as athletes, we have this super-powerful platform and we know the power of social media, and it was during COVID, so together we created the list and then posted it on social media." It was instantly picked up by high-profile websites such as ESPN and other athletes with huge platforms. Logan says the list had such viral velocity "because people care about what we're talking about. People were starting to react to it, and

·that's when the administration set some time to have the conversation about all the things that we asked for."

The administration thoughtfully considered each item on the list, including the controversial demand to replace the century-plus-old alma mater. The decision to keep the song while the committee studied its history kept the controversy in an unsettled state. A small number of athletes on university scholarships garnered much attention across social media by saying they were considering sitting out and not playing their respective sports. The phenomenon of collegiate athletes modeling professional athletes by finding their voices was not unique to UT; across the country, they began to use their power, individually and collectively, to effect change at their own schools. Students, including athletes and band members, protested, and online groups across the country, many unaffiliated with UT, joined in the global outcry for reform, outrage, and protest.

Many alumni were outraged by the students' demand to drop their beloved alma mater. They overwhelmingly pushed back against the students' demands, without any dialogue, decrying what they saw as cancel culture being used to take away something very dear to them while forever changing the school's culture. To some, it became a classic conflict, balancing the desire to protect deeply held tradition versus erasing history in an epic, high-profile clash that was perceived to be between black and white, right and left, and, perhaps most importantly, young and old.

The playing field had become a cultural battlefield between not just students and administration but also a state and country that were deeply divided and unable to engage in any form of civil discourse. The eyes of the state were laser-focused on this battle, along with those of universities and media across the country and world, all carefully watching the university's response and approach.

Although outsiders wanted to simplify the issues by making the dispute about current students and faculty versus the more than 540,000 alumni, things were far more nuanced and complex. National public relations and crisis firms recommended to replace the song. Deutser differed from these firms by creating a multidimensional plan to work *within* the decision to keep the song in place while the commission could study its history.

It quickly became clear, however, that the real need was to listen to and engage the multitude of diverse voices offering opinions on "The Eyes of Texas"—including the angriest and most hostile ones. While the song was the catalyst, it revealed that the investigation needed to address and answer a potentially deeper-seated problem affecting not just this university but schools across the country. This could only be accomplished by opening the process to allow the full spectrum of vulnerable and raw emotions to be expressed. The model Deutser created and facilitated for this process has since become a model for addressing complex social issues of all kinds on campuses nationwide. As Logan recalls, "I think you built trust by listening and saying, 'There is no right or wrong, we're just here to discuss the idea that we're discussing.' And I've actually taken your approach into other situations." Our role was never to convince or orchestrate an outcome, but to listen and allow one to emerge.

Listening Without Labels Was the Game Changer

The first interviews were the turning point for me. It was not simply the words repeated over and over that expressed frustration from those I interviewed—"you don't belong here," "you are white," "you are old," and "I can't believe they sent us another white guy to talk about race." It was clear that their pent-up bias needed to come out, and as we entered into discourse and asked more thoughtful questions, their answers became deeper and more connected, as did their own questions. The key was recognizing that people with wildly different perspectives, attached to deeply held belief systems yet lacking any voice, needed an outlet. The incendiary nature of the controversy had a velocity that begged for a forum that would host an honest exchange—even if that forum was one person with the authority and willingness to listen.

At first the discussions were fueled by hate, but by listening and challenging feelings, with a focus on facts, all parties gave discourse and genuine connection some space to evolve. The interviewees wanted to be heard. The university wanted them to be heard. This process allowed everyone to come back to the table with historical perspective, bridged relationships, and important facts.

LEADERSHIP OF BELONGING

While the interviews and study continued, UT was losing the public relations battle, with ugly, anger-inciting stories swirling that resorted to labeling the entirety of the alumni, and especially its donors, as racist, furthering the divide with current students. I was asked by many, "How does it feel to be losing on something as important as the Eyes?" And "Do you think the president can remain if he can't win this argument?" The response was the same over and over: this work wasn't about winning or losing, but rather about finding the truth and the chance to "give people space to make their own decisions." The president shared that just because people disagree, it doesn't mean they don't belong. He was less concerned with appeasing or responding to the loudest on either extreme of the controversy and more with putting his energy into the people stuck in the middle who yearned for information and better understanding. His goal was to determine the facts about the history of the song and share that information in a way that allowed people to feel comfortable deciding about the tradition for themselves.

The months-long process of engaging conversation generated feelings of inclusiveness and made way for an openness to receive and review the fifty-eight-page "Eyes of Texas" report (www.eyesoftexas .utexas.edu) on the alma mater. The process worked to bring all closer to the middle where they could consider the findings of the report, which was transparent and filled with facts to support many diverse opinion sets. It talked in great detail about the song's authors and origins, including inputs and original documentation provided by the author's granddaughters; details about the first performance; and its many uses over the generations to fight racism over the past hundred years. The report highlighted facts and gave historical context—and demonstrated how the song reflects the history of America.

The report also showed the complexity of racial understanding today. After it was published, and more than fifty presentations were made to groups to invite discussion and encourage greater understanding of its content, the song gained new meaning when more than a hundred thousand people stood and sang it together loudly and proudly at the 2021 football season's opening game (and every sports event thereafter). There were also a handful of individuals who respectfully chose to stand but not sing—as was their choice. Our goal was to give information and allow people to make their own personal choices. It worked. More importantly, the song and the work around it became a vehicle of change on campus as names of buildings were changed and new funding was appropriated to create opportunities for underserved students and to reach underserved communities. Funds were also allotted for student athletes and band members to direct to organizations effecting social change. UT was able to thoughtfully respond and begin to move forward. Through its actions, people could come together to share priorities that once divided many. They moved from derision to cooperation; now, individuals and groups could express disagreement yet still collaborate toward common goals for the betterment of the university, its students, and the broader community.

Asked if there was one thing that should have been done differently, Logan Eggleston, the student leader who launched this inquiry through the initial list of demands, replied, "I don't know if I would do anything differently because I'm really happy with where we are now.

But I think I would have pressed harder to have those real conversations with people with different perspectives sooner. There were a lot of emails sent around with the administration and I wish we could have had a time where we came together, with the donors, with those people who sent the emails, with the Precursors, with older black athletes, older white athletes, and had a conversation about what the song means to them. We don't always have to have the same opinion, but we can respect other people. And that's what it all comes down to, respecting other people's identity, perspective, and opinions. You don't always have to agree, but it's okay to just be nice and show respect. And I feel if we had that time to sit down and be able to understand some of the other people's relationships to the song, and then they were able to understand my relationship to the song, you know, a lot of the tension would have totally gone away."

At times during the process she became frustrated by the pace of change, even threatening to go to the media to garner support and accelerate matters. I said to her, "You can go to the media if you want. But you already have earned a seat at the table and have the loudest voice in the room." I continued, "Real and lasting change takes time—it is your choice." She chose instead to go deep into the process, seeking long-term change and not the quick fix.

In the end, we all learned that labeling is dangerous. Sometimes we are so passionate and feel so pressured to represent others that we take away our power to be part of the conversation and actually listen. We even forget to listen when we are asking for people to do just that. Then the agenda takes over, leaving little space for the discourse. And, the discourse on complicated issues, like this, will inevitably continue with future generations wanting their own opportunity to understand and reflect on history.

LABELS

First, spend some time and review the **LABELS** on the opposite page. The list of labels is not exhaustive, but simply meant to spur your thinking. Use those terms to help inform your answers to these questions.

Identify ten ways people label you.

1. Which labels are accurate? Why?

_____
_____
_____

2. Which labels are not accurate? Why?

_____
_____
_____

Identify five ways you label yourself.

1. Which labels are accurate? Why?

_____
_____
_____

2. Which labels are not accurate? Why?

_____
_____
_____
_____

Which labels are the most used, the most appropriate, and most limiting?

_____
_____

Which labels do you focus on more: internal or external? Why? _____

_____

Do labels matter to you? Why or why not? How do you hope to be labeled?

_____
_____

Can good ever come from labeling others? Why or why not? _____

_____

HELLO MY NAME IS

HELLO MY NAME IS

HELLO MY NAME IS

HELLO MY NAME IS

HELLO MY NAME IS

HELLO MY NAME IS

HELLO MY NAME IS

HELLO MY NAME IS

HELLO MY NAME IS

HELLO MY NAME IS

LABELS

AGGRESSIVE	EDUCATED	LIBERAL	ROLE MODEL
ALLY	ELITIST	LISTENER	SELFLESS
AMBITIOUS	EMPATHETIC	LOSER	SENSITIVE
AMERICAN	ENEMY	MAJORITY	SEXIST
ANGRY	EXTREMIST	MANAGER	SHORT
ANXIOUS	FAT	MENTOR	SIBLING
ASIAN	FATHER	MILLENNIAL	SKINNY
ASSERTIVE	FEMINIST	MINORITY	SMART
ATHEIST	FIT	MOTHER	SNOWFLAKE
ATHLETE	FOLLOWER	MOTIVATED	SOUTHERNER
AUNT	FRIEND	MUSLIM	SPIRITUAL
AVOIDANT	FRIENDLY	NATIONALITY	SPOUSE
BIPOC	FUNNY	NEIGHBOR	STRAIGHT
BLACK	GAMER	NICE	STRESSED
BOOMER	GAY	NORMAL	STUBBORN
BOSS	GEN X	NORTHERNER	STUDENT
CALM	GEN Z	OLD	TALL
CAPABLE	GRANDPARENT	OPTIMIST	TEACHER
CARETAKER	HAPPY	OUTSPOKEN	TOLERANT
CARING	HEALTHY	OVERWEIGHT	TRANS
CHILD	HELPFUL	PARENT	TYPE A
CHRISTIAN	HINDU	PEER	TYPE B
CHURCH-GOER	HISPANIC	PEOPLE PLEASER	UGLY
CLIENT	HONEST	PERFECTIONIST	UNCLE
CLUELESS	HUMAN	PESSIMIST	UNINFORMED
COLLEAGUE	HUSBAND	POOR	UNRELIABLE
CONFIDENT	HYPER	PRETTY	VISIONARY
CONSERVATIVE	ILL	PRIVILEGED	WEIRD
CREATIVE	INDEPENDENT	QUIET	WHITE
CRITICAL	INTELLIGENT	RACIST	WIFE
DEMOCRAT	JEWISH	RADICAL	WINNER
DEPRESSED	JUNIOR	RATIONAL	WORKING MOTHER
DETERMINED	LEADER	REPUBLICAN	YOUNG
DRIVEN	LEFT-LEANING	RICH	
DUMB	LESBIAN	RIGHT-LEANING	

LABELING ROBS US OF INDIVIDUALITY

Your individual need to be seen and heard for your perspective, which combines your knowledge, experience, understanding, and personal grace, allows you to act as a whole human. By contrast, a label reduces you to just one thing. As we strive to understand one another more fully, begin noticing the labels that others apply to you and that you apply to others. When we rush to judgment, we've already taken something from another, impeding their ability to reveal themselves deeply and fully in ways labels can't express. Such a sprint can seem innocuous and harmless, masquerading as the fact that you've already gotten the point and don't need to listen to someone, because you already know what they will say, think, or represent. But that is a falsehood and also the entry point to ongoing resistance and resentment without resolution or shared resolution. Standing in your supreme spot of "knowing" can leave just you there—alone. Or if not alone, it can wall you inside an echo chamber, accompanied by others who share the same labels and reductionist thought, open only to discourse with those who support your position and use the same words and labels. This keeps your group in and another out. Since all belonging is built on positivity and inclusion, you must actively release your lifelong habits of labeling and instead make openness and active listening the start of your own personal listening tour. Without labels, of course.

Chapter 3

IT'S NOT ONE THING, IT'S THE OTHER

Belonging Rule #3: **CHOOSE IDENTITY OVER PURPOSE**

P urpose has been an often-used buzzword for the past few decades. Savvy organizations figured out that they could unite a group of people by rallying them around something they all cared deeply about or wanted to invest in, be it their time and energy, money and attention, or simple support. Leaders were challenged to ask themselves about their "why." It became accepted practice to keep driving yourself not just to succeed but for the purpose behind or associated with that success. It became accepted business wisdom to believe that purpose drives results. And it does.

Many business writers and scholars acknowledge that leveraging purpose can lead to profound outcomes. But having purpose as an organization's main driver can create imbalances, self-righteousness, and elitism, as its highest goals are reserved for only the most fervently dedicated. The end result: silos of zealous participants who set a standard that others cannot meet. Instead, our research with tens of thousands of individuals in hundreds of companies shows that prioritizing identity as a whole over narrowly focusing on purpose cultivates deeper organizational roots, and that purpose is only one element that serves to help us find our fit, value our work, and believe in the team. Believing in the reason you are doing something is not the same as believing in the people you are doing it with. To some, our emphasis on identity over purpose may seem like a nuanced concept or perspective. But it is a critical one. The much-hailed purpose is no doubt a vital part of a greater, more influential organizational identity equation. It brings grounding to it, but alone it cannot drive it forward or create the lasting differentiation for an organization. Ideally, in companies that foster belonging, both beliefs are abundant. But by leading with identity, you are much more likely to create wholeness, inclusion, and belonging than you are by leading with only purpose.

Let's take a closer look at this belonging dynamic with a concept that we often forget—you have a choice. As a leader, you have a choice of what you prioritize, and what you choose will determine the quality of your interactions, what you focus on, and likely whether you enjoy your day. Many leaders start with purpose—their daybreak battle cry and raison d'être, which serves to remind them that there is a deeper reason for the daily grind beyond reasonable or even extraordinary success. And purpose is important, vitally important. But, like so much of the conversation with belonging, where purpose sits in the organization can deeply impact how belonging takes shape. If, as conventional wisdom suggests, purpose is our everything, then we are missing the big thing—identity. Purpose therefore can no longer be thought of as in the lead, but rather genuinely serving a higher purpose: identity. That takes us to **Belonging Rule #3: *Choose Identity over Purpose.***

My goal here is to make the case for collective, shared identity—not your own. Every concept I will discuss here is designed to facilitate and increase belonging, not division. So please discard all the arguments you are about to make to defend purpose or attempt to prioritize your personal identity. You can always do that later. Instead, I want to challenge you again to eliminate labels—even for yourself—while reading this chapter. Think about the version of identity I'm putting forth as your macro-organizational identity: your company, your religious home, your organizations, your team, your extended family, and so on. I'm not talking about identity through a lens of what we as individuals identify as or with. Rather, this is about a greater identity—the collective identity.

You won't need to leave your entire personal identity at the door. Rather, I will ask you to consider how you want it to show up, while recognizing your desire to be part of something bigger than you. What we're here to consider is your participation in the action of the whole. This is what it means to fit in and belong. Having agreement around identity is fundamental to belonging as it provides the most solid, well-thought-out framework for understanding personal motivations and drivers within the context of organizational environments.

At Deutser, we define organizational identity through the broader organizational lens as being made up of values, characteristics, traditions, rituals, beliefs, and shared behavioral competencies, as well as expectations. And, of course, purpose is also a key part of our definition. Identity is the lifeblood and DNA of any organization. Identity comprises the things that we see, feel, experience, and ultimately choose whether to be a part of—the defining elements of any organization, no matter how small or large. Together, this collection of things is more important than any one element in determining true ability to belong. If it is naturally part of an identity, then it can be naturally and authentically accepted into the organization.

In our framework, these are the elements of identity:

Purpose: The glue that binds people together in support of a common cause, often linking each individual's goals with those of the organization. Purpose answers these questions: Why do we exist? What needs do we fill? Why do we do what we do?

Characteristics: The central attributes of the organization; what makes the organization distinctive and therefore unique among other organizations; and what employees perceive to be enduring or continuing, regardless of objective changes in the organizational environment.

Values: The beliefs that an organization's members hold in common, from which they derive a shared sense of direction and motivation. They form the foundation on which you perform work and conduct yourself. Values guide people, creating a shared mental model of how employees think and act.

Behavioral Competencies: Purposeful actions that shape an organization's identity from the bottom-up. Behavioral competencies create a tangible link between who the organization is, what it values, and what it expects to achieve. Explicitly defined, they show employees what success looks like, mitigating tendencies toward biased judgments by allowing everyone to clearly understand the critical competencies and specific behavioral examples underlying the organization's culture, so they know how to champion it. By providing behavioral examples for how best to approach daily work, employees are galvanized around not only shared beliefs, but also individual actions.

Traditions: The rituals, celebrations, and practices that bring people together across the organization, traditions are timeless ways to honor the organization's culture and connect employees through shared experiences. They include things like annual holiday parties or celebrations for staff anniversaries, and reward and recognition programs to coincide with individual or collective milestones. Traditions reflect precious practices, ways in which organizational members can get together in acknowledgment, respect, and joy. As the organization evolves, so may its many traditions, but they should always be considered as precious practices that create a captivating and powerful culture of belonging.

Each element of identity relates to and is reliant on the rest. While each component is vital to the full picture, there is a hierarchy to their interactions. The relationships between values and behavioral expectations are the nucleus of the organization. They are the defining elements of "how we do things around here." We think of values as the "WE" in the organizational identity equation—the things that, together, we all strive for and work to achieve. On the other side of the coin are the behavioral expectations, perhaps the most misunderstood and misused tool a leader has for setting expectations and norming the organization and its leadership, management, and workforce. Behaviors are the organizational "ME"—the daily things that every individual can work on and be held accountable for. They protect organizations and increase belonging because they build the social contract for how we are expected to act and interact. The WE and the ME help to facilitate belonging in organizations.

Identity, properly constructed and accessed, bolsters a leader's confidence, not with catchy phrasing or workshop mantras but with solid information upon which they can rely in the most high-pressure moments. At Deutser, we teach leaders to lead with their whole being, never stepping out of the fight while finding deep fulfillment through challenge and partnership with others. We train leaders how to build trust and be worthy of that trust. We help leaders withstand any storm and stand up for what they believe in—which may differ from the cause or movement of the moment. We model how to resist convenient answers that may represent a projected purpose in alignment with data points. Identity work leads to lasting, accepted, and adopted change.

THE ECOSYSTEM OF BELONGING

We look at the interconnectedness of identity and all its elements. We think about them as elements of a periodic table. They come together in an intentionally created and aligned ecosystem of elements that inform the company's DNA.

At the heart of the ecosystem is belonging. It is the element that undeniably connects, protects, and ensures how the values and behaviors work together to ensure the organization is true to who it says it is: its identity.

If you think about some of the most visible brands, clear associations to identity quickly come to mind. You immediately understand what it means to be Nike, Coca-Cola, or Apple. You have expectations for interacting with them that stem from their unique identities. Organizations that are disconnected from their identities often don't deliver on promises to their customers or employees and ultimately fail. They lack cohesion and authenticity—and no organization can compensate for a lack of authenticity.

Identity is our foundation. Its strength and clarity determine our success and longevity. So, why is identity so underutilized? I have multiple hypotheses. First, many want to take shortcuts to building identity. They see it as a nice-to-have, but a hard-to-create. It is easier to disaggregate each of the elements and think of them as standalones. I would argue that is why most organizations stop at purpose (or mission). There is also an over-confidence gap. Leaders often see their identity as clearly defined, but merely talking about identity doesn't translate to people living and owning it. After all, leaders tell us, "We are wildly successful," "We are in our hundredth year," or "We are leaders in our industry." These all may be true, but your employees may have very different perspectives on this. This misalignment is another place where employees and people begin to feel even the micro-cracks in their relationship with their employer, place of worship, or clubs. People on the front lines know when things are working their best and when they

ECOSYSTEM OF BELONGING

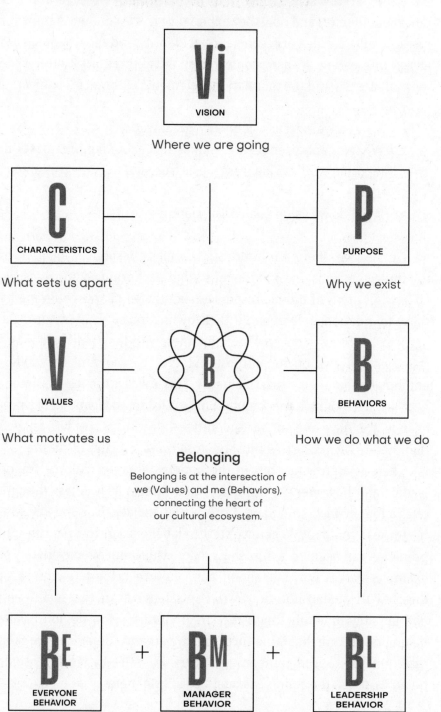

Vi
VISION
Where we are going

C
CHARACTERISTICS
What sets us apart

P
PURPOSE
Why we exist

V
VALUES
What motivates us

B

B
BEHAVIORS
How we do what we do

Belonging
Belonging is at the intersection of
we (Values) and me (Behaviors),
connecting the heart of
our cultural ecosystem.

B^E
EVERYONE
BEHAVIOR

+

B^M
MANAGER
BEHAVIOR

+

B^L
LEADERSHIP
BEHAVIOR

are off. What they sense is the difference between how organizations talk about identity and how they experience it. We conduct significant research into the idea of organizational identity, and the responses are always interesting. We ask people to respond to three questions on the topic of identity and the foundational elements of their companies:

1. Why do we exist as a company/organization?
2. What is central, enduring, and distinct about our organization (in other words, what was true, is true, and must be true about us)?
3. What do we value as an organization?

On average, there are hundreds of unique responses for each of the three questions. Even in the most high-performing companies, we collect hundreds of unique responses about what people believe to be these foundational elements in their own companies. Many of these participants work in successful companies, with long-held values and statements of mission and purpose. Yet, their people think very different things about their shared elements. This is where the "Great Disconnect" begins—right at the foundation. As a leader navigating the sea of change, you have one anchor—identity—but your people will tell you that there is a gap, one that must be closed, and it relates to culture.

There is a growing shift in the understanding of culture among leaders and how identity influences and directs it. It is less thought of as a touchy-feely thing and more as a financial driver and key connector in a company. When we start to label our culture, we run into problems and begin to diminish its macro value and effectiveness. For example, leaders may talk about safety culture, belonging culture, or diverse culture. But how do you have a safety culture that is different and possibly in conflict with the larger culture? How do you have a belonging culture that is distinct from the organizational culture? You cannot do both. And companies that try will fail—by leaving people out or worse, in the context of safety, by killing them.

Culture is how we do things and is directed and connected by our identity. It would be easy for me to create a safety culture that ensures no accidents—by ceasing to do business. But that makes no sense. It conflicts with our purpose and why we exist. By all means, create a culture that drives safety, but ensure it is part of the macro view of what your organization collectively strives to achieve. Your identity sets your culture; your culture directs your actions; your actions keep you performing at the highest levels.

What you do with your identity will determine your openness toward and belief in creating a company that values belonging. Without an identity, you are simply bolting parts and pieces onto your company that are not natural. You are telling your employees, customers, members, and fans what is and what is not important—and even the important add-ons can easily be removed with any significant leadership change. If you fail to include belonging—the concept, if not necessarily the exact word—in the definitions, expectations, and actions at your organization's core, and you don't measure it regularly, your company will never live up to its full belonging potential. You will be leaving people out, whether intentionally or unintentionally, and will not be aware of the disconnection and disengagement that exists. Worse, you will not be living up to your full potential, and neither will your people.

Purpose in Its Place

So why do leaders lead with purpose? Purpose is important. Some of the greatest thought leaders as well as military leaders will argue no principle is higher. And they are right—on paper. Purpose rests at the very top of our cultural ecosystem. It is a foundational element of any company and, I would argue, any person. When we envision purpose in a siloed structure, it becomes disconnected from the whole. The ecosystem requires (and helps to provide) a purposeful connectivity to the other elements that illuminate and bring purpose to life and into proportion. People must have purpose; so must their organizations.

Without purpose, both will be untethered and float aimlessly, searching for the unattainable. We can only grasp the unattainable when we are clear on our purpose. Purpose feeds understanding about who we are and the direction in which we are going.

Although I don't believe leaders should begin any question with the word "why" (I will describe through the rest of the book how it creates division and pits people against each other), I do also understand that purpose is our collective "why." But, when we ask another why something occurred or why they think it is important, it creates an immediate disconnect as the brain scrambles to find a solid defense, even if it's for something positive. "Why" makes us feel like we're on the line for something, even an explanation. We will delve into this aspect of "why" in chapter four; here, we are exploring more of the "why we exist" question. Understand for now that we feel under a certain amount of pressure to produce a good answer. It is grossly over-discussed, under-considered, and misunderstood.

Some will talk about purpose, others about mission, and some will talk about both. I view purpose as a higher-order element that absorbs the concept of a mission. Most companies have well-crafted and often wordy statements of purpose designed to appease or address every constituency. They are compliant in that they exist; they are publicly facing and also shared with employees. Rarely, however, do they connect to the heart and soul of the workforce, unless they are more inward- and human-facing mission-driven macro statements. Few mission or purpose statements inspire me, not even those from educational or healthcare institutions, which profess to change lives and the world. They are noble, but rarely human or real. And if it is so difficult simply to compose a statement that captures the spirit of what you are trying to accomplish, imagine how hard it is actually to achieve it.

A DIFFERENTIATED APPROACH TO IDENTITY

This gets to the core of the inverse thinking behind purpose and identity. Identity is complex and layered. But identity is what makes us—and what makes our pursuit of delineating our purpose meaningful and unique. When we relate our purpose to our identity, this purpose statement somehow seems more within reach. If we think about purpose as our "why" and our "what," then identity is our "who" and our "how." The "who" and the "how" speak to the way leaders and their workforce will bring the organization's identity to life. How will this be achieved? In what ways will leaders uniquely give it life through their actions, selection of talent, and feelings they evoke or inspire in others? Purpose is necessary but not sufficient in creating identity—you need the other elements to come together in a coherent manner to cultivate the shared agreements that embed belonging.

Consider the National Football League. The NFL comprises thirty-two teams. They all play on the same size field. They have the same salary requirements and caps, they each have coaches, trainers, and a stadium where they play. NFL teams have similar purposes. They exist to provide world-class entertainment. They exist to win and bring Super Bowl championships home to their city and fans. They exist to create and support community. In other words, the uniformity among them is striking. We know what to expect when we watch or attend a football game. This is true in other professional sports, too. The familiar parts of Major League Baseball or any other sport on that level have been crafted through consistent design and the rules of the game.

So, if purpose is the only thing, how can one team rise above? Or, said differently, how can each of the thirty-two teams distinguish themselves from one another when at their core they share similar purposes? Has one fulfilled their purpose and the other thirty-one have not?

We can debate that answer, speculating about how each team may identify with their role in the ecosphere that exists to support it—or we can accept simply that identity is their differentiator. Not the identity defined by their logo, colors, or city/regional name—those comprise our surface perception. I mean the identity they create through the purpose, values, behaviors, characteristics, and traditions that define them and ultimately their success. Sadly, this is as true of low-performing teams as it is of high-performing teams. Identity cannot be faked or contrived. Losing teams are often untethered from their identity and left adrift, resulting in lackluster results and a plunge to last place.

While the focus of this rule is of a differentiated, shared identity, we also recognize the role the leader plays in creating, protecting, and living out that identity. Therefore, we as leaders—both as individuals and as the heads of organizations, companies, teams, and families—need to think about how our broader personal view of identity aligns with that of the organization or group we are leading. How do we think about our own values and behavioral expectations for ourselves and others in our personal and professional ecosystems? Which traditions are the most defining? Take time to think about this through the lens of you as a leader. Think about your influence on identity and its influence on you.

When you make a differentiated identity the foundation of the organization, selecting the elements that define your culture, you fundamentally reset expectations for you and everyone around you. There's no longer a question or debate over what you stand for and expect in any key area. You have provided clarity. For instance, think about how organizations broadly proclaim their commitment to diversity. You cannot commit to diversity without making belonging part of your identity. Nor can you commit to diversity without making inclusivity part of your DNA. The concepts you choose will define your ultimate outcomes. You can always hire a DEI coordinator, but if belonging is not part of your value set, they will fail. DEI initiatives fail at tremendous rates because organizations don't bond with the values and accept them at their core. The organizational organism will always reject the foreign object trying to force itself in. The work of diversity—or any sort of personal or organizational differentiation—must come from the inside, and that inside is identity.

Perhaps because of my love of history, or my time living and working in London at a solicitors' (legal) firm early in my career, I have a connection to and deep curiosity about the English monarchy. I was therefore touched by its response to an episode in the palace—most of which was appropriate. The story: A British citizen attended an event at Buckingham Palace and was greeted with an uncomfortable round of questions about where she was from by a member of the family. Her first response was, "I am from England." The questioner continued, obviously not satisfied that this woman was of English descent because of any of several possible reasons, including the color of her skin, name, clothing, or dialect. As the conversation deteriorated, the visitor repeated that she was a British citizen and that members of her family had immigrated from the Caribbean and Africa.

The report was shocking and horrifying—who asks that question, much less thinks it? How this story relates to belonging is not in the ignorance and insensitivity of the questioner, but the root issue illuminated in the Royal Household's responses. Most were expected and appropriate: the questioner's resignation, the family distancing them, and a statement of disappointment and apology. But they also included a statement that reinforced and reminded people of the Household's diversity and inclusivity policies. What? Were they governing human behavior though policy? It is a cultural issue. It is a human issue. It is an identity issue. *Policy* only sets a standard; *culture* norms behavior. When someone refers to a policy, they are clearly stating it, but not necessarily living it. Businesses make this same error across the globe daily. People make mistakes, and the organization pushes the policy. What this says is that at the very core, the organization needs to ask itself real questions to examine, understand, and evolve its identity.

In this exercise, you'll reflect on the foundational elements of your personal and collective cultural ecosystems—vision, purpose, values, characteristics, and behaviors. After you're finished, reflect on areas that are in sync or in discord. What needs to happen to align your individual identity with the collective "we" identity in your organization?

ME
BELONGING

Where I am going (VISION)

Why I exist (PURPOSE)

What is important to me (VALUES)

What sets me apart (CHARACTERISTICS)

What habits support me best (BEHAVIORS)

Why do we exist (PURPOSE)

Where are we going (VISION)

**What sets us apart
(CHARACTERISTICS)**

**What is important to the team
(VALUES)**

**What habits support us best
(BEHAVIORS)**

THE BATTLE OVER IDENTITY

Penney Ainsworth certainly demonstrates her values. The former director of the Boys & Girls Club in Jackson, Mississippi, Penney describes
her work as service. Why is this so important? Because Boys & Girls
Clubs—and the kids' parents—are competing for that sense of belonging with gangs—gangs who do show up, gangs who always make you
feel like you belong so that you to do what they want you to do. She
consistently demonstrates her dedication to a group of young people
who have little exposure to the world beyond "the four square blocks"
where they live.

At first glance, you might think it's great that kids have somewhere
to go after school where they can play sports, spend time with friends,
perhaps stay out of trouble, or not be alone while waiting for a working parent to come home. Now understand for a moment that these
same kids are being left on their own. Penney tells us that they don't
have confidence that any adult is going to show up for them. No adult
is going to consistently follow through on something asked about or
promised. No adult is going to hold them accountable for where they
are or what they do. Given this lack of confidence, for something to give
them a sense of belonging that extends beyond their street smarts and
self-efficacy, it must get their attention and stimulate a response that
says, "I want to be here."

To win the confidence of these kids, Penney started where we
at Deutser so often start: by creating belonging. The physical space
was her first challenge. Penney tells us, "The building was horrible
looking—nasty. The food was bad." Penney worked to improve the
building so kids could begin to see and feel that they were worthy
of the best things in life, not what was abandoned, neglected, and
dilapidated—because how could that appeal, versus being a cool insider
with a gang? Her organization began to create an environment where
they could see more and do more. She and the other leaders committed to showing up for the kids when they needed them and when they

didn't. They all had Penney's cell number. The leaders introduced kids to increasing possibility. The kids were given the chance to play soccer and listen to music. Penney brought in tutors and started talking with them about college. She eventually took some students on a week-long college tour, visiting three states over six days. Penney showed them a world beyond their "four square blocks." They could see something bigger that they could join and participate in, a place where they could show up for each other and begin to create shared identity.

Even more impressive, these kids took the belonging skills Penney taught them home, where they demanded the same kind of accountability and more consistency. One expectation of the program was that the kids had to pay their advantage forward. They therefore learned to be part of a community. The program also emphasized making better choices. If the outcome and consequences for one choice or set of choices wasn't what the kids wanted, they had adults to help them define better choices that might lead to better outcomes. They were always expected to be part of the group.

Some of Penney's takeaways for creating that special sense of belonging include the following:

1. Talk to the kids, not at them.
2. Listen more than anyone. Make sure they are heard.
3. Give them opportunities for power and influence as well as some control over what they are doing.
4. Make sure they know that choice is what drives an increasingly better life. Better choices give you more to choose from.
5. Expose people to things outside of their "four blocks."

Penney passionately believes that through a trusting relationship with even *one* adult, a child's world opens. The key to this is to "do what you say and say what you'll do." When a child can see more, they begin to believe they can do more. Take the same concepts and expand them to your organization, your company, and your family. Think about the increased connections and the spaces you open up for them to be part of something bigger than themselves. It is not just Penney's kids who are searching for it—it is the workforce and all of us.

VALUES THAT INSPIRE

Values are critical—the very backbone of an organization's identity. So, why are companies going to the lowest common denominator when it comes to composing them? Simply stated, the go-to, one-word values do not work. Period. They lack meaning, they lack intention, they lack heart and soul—they lack connection. They also show the organization's lack of commitment. They serve as a giant compliant stamp on the forehead of the company. They look silly and out of place.

Research by Gallup shows that workers do not absorb the typical single-word values many organizations espouse. According to their findings, only 27% of employees believe in their companies. They are what they are: flat, single words that give people too many ways to define them (even when the company provides a definition). They are so overused and generic that they no longer have meaning or evoke a reaction—precisely what values are intended to do. The compliant values—honesty, integrity, humility, family, team, diversity, and so on—are no more than isolated terms with definitions to which everyone can assign their own narrative. And our research shows that is exactly what they do.

When leaders gravitate toward these sorts of terms, we always challenge them to consider what they mean and how they want people to think and act. Leaders often agree on the words but rarely take the time to think about their full meanings and implications. This gap creates an opportunity for people to do what they *think* we say, versus what we mean.

Leaders must always be interested in the conversation and, ultimately, the debate, within leadership teams around core values and organizational characteristics. It is why our process consistently involves the whole of the organization and getting the perspective of the entire workforce.

Family as a Value

One of the places where conflict over identity occurs is in the conversation about "family" as a value. It is natural for leaders, especially in smaller to mid-sized organizations, to gravitate to the feeling that they want to model "family" in some way. On the surface, leaders feel good about creating an environment they believe people will want to be part of. From an organizational standpoint, they think about family as a place where people take care of each other and where the company takes care of the people. This sounds caring and good to most leaders.

On deeper inspection, however, families are also complex entities, far different from high-functioning teams. Family members can behave almost any way they want, knowing they may disenfranchise themselves temporarily but remain family regardless. Members of teams lack this leeway; not only must they coexist but also overcome differences and thrive together. It is why we encourage the debate among leaders between the concepts of family and team, which initially seem very similar. Only in rare cases will we push for family as an organizational value over team.

This is even true in family-owned and multigenerational companies. We have heads of family who will fiercely fight for their kin, but what they really may be advocating for is a high-functioning team. As generations evolve, so, too, do the challenges inherent in growing families. In fact, the very things that hold families together are the same things that can create the greatest conflict within them.

Take a family-owned company transitioning from the first generation to the second and now needing to prepare the third. Everyone is strongly connected to the founder and their perceptions of his vision and how he led—albeit in a different time more than two decades ago. Generation two saw firsthand how he led and the sort of demands, often unreasonable, he placed on them. Generation three was more removed and was the recipient of his grandfatherly love. Both later generations experienced "family," but how they experienced it and their views of how to sustain the family's success are far different. So, too, are their expectations for how the company should "maintain their shared values"—even when they were not experienced or shared in the same way.

Such differences in perception are magnified when we remove the generational label (first, second, or third) and realize the generations are made up of individuals who happen to be part of the same or extended family. In other words, these generations, or individuals within them, may say or appear to say the same things, but the meanings they ascribe to the company's values may be very different. This is magnified when the expectations around the values are passed to the CEO to lead through. To his credit, the CEO has worked to understand the family's values, while also shifting them to meet the demands of the business today and for the next generation. That means change—but necessary and healthy change—right at the core of the organization and its identity.

Today's leaders must be ready to confront such generational struggles, both in family-owned companies and successful non-family companies with long-tenured CEOs, while appreciating and possibly updating the organization's identity. Should they embrace the full past of the organization or amplify the need for purposeful change? Some leaders are unwilling to decide, but the right answer will be vital for the organization's long-term survival. Too often, a board or family will believe the biggest decision they need to make is simply choosing a successor. In reality, the big decision is to choose a successor while helping them navigate pitfalls that appear early in their tenure. This is often a forgotten responsibility—as the leader is regularly hired and left to fend for themselves from day one. Thus, it is critical to start by empowering the leader to make a deep study of the organization's identity—they will be the captain of it going forward and will not cede that duty to the family or others. The leader must know for themselves what the identity is and not solely rely on others to provide the definition. Leaders who are overly swift to give in to these constituencies on questions of identity are never able to get the necessary grounding for their leadership. Instead, the new leader must understand for themselves what is real—not simply accept what a family or board tells them is real—then champion any changes needed. That may require shedding any of the institution's past that is no longer relevant to where the leader is or where they need to guide the organization. It is that important.

Deutser's Humanized Values

I am embarrassed when I think back on the origins of my company. We did amazing things in some of the most complex and controversial areas, producing unbelievable outcomes. Yet, we were not living our best lives or near our full potential. It serves no one to look back and ask the reasons why I did what I did—after all, I knew what the highest-performing companies needed and did to sustain success. I intentionally assembled an elite group of wildly talented people in different areas of expertise, and I learned about their often-competing backgrounds: management consultants, social scientists, PhDs, organizational psychologists and anthropologists, elite designers and creative thinkers, and experiential and engagement experts. No one saw the world through the same lens.

I thought it was great, but I failed to recognize the friction that I had caused through this recruitment style. Everyday work was being relentlessly challenged through very different world, business, and academic lenses. The chaos was human made—or as my team called it, Brad made. It was so dysfunctional that I scheduled myself out of the office eight hours every day, choosing instead to work at night until the wee hours of the morning. Instead of turning into the power (or dysfunction), I retreated from it and circumvented it. The most talented and brilliant people were the ones who were most entrenched in their ways—and who thus caused the greatest friction with me.

Things didn't change until several of my leaders came to me and said, "We are experts at identity—this is what we do for others. Why can't we do it for us?" Not wanting more conflict, and believing we shared enough commonality, I acquiesced and put the company through our own process. The result: we tripled the size of the company, achieved financial stability, reset the growth trajectory, opened three new businesses, and published one best-selling book. But it is not the result that sustains us. It is the work and the way we made it ours, by humanizing it and genuinely connecting it with the heart and soul of our people—and, in turn, their connecting with me. We defined our vision and our purpose and saved the most contentious discussions for our values and behaviors. There were tears, raised voices, and vocal disagreements until we agreed on who we were and wanted to become. Yet, it literally changed everything—from the paint color on our front door, to our interactions with each other, to who could stay in our company and who would self-select out or be asked to leave.

Part of the dysfunction was created by our earliest set of values. They were the antithesis of Deutser and hardly human. They were simply word values until we addressed and began the process to humanize them and make them ours.

Our early values:

- Entrepreneurial
- Results oriented
- Creative
- Continuous improvement/change
- Communicate/team
- Passion

We breathed some life into the values to humanize them, and now they not only embody the best of us, but they also direct our people and connect our actions:

- Think like an entrepreneur
- Embrace and lead change
- Create collaboratively
- Design for impact
- Love what we do, and it shows

We supported our values with a set of behavioral expectations for every employee—regardless of their title or role in the company.

Our Everyone Behaviors

- Igniting creativity
- Navigating ambiguity
- Listening with heart
- Winning collectively
- Delivering the WOW!

And we created an overarching philosophy that described what we collectively believe.

Our Philosophy and Beliefs

- We love to help.
- We embrace change.
- We are intentionally human.
- We are original in all we do.
- We are united by our differences.

These form the core of our identity. We don't state belonging or inclusion in our words, but we do in our definitions and interactions and in how we are united by difference. It rests at the center of our ecosystem. Belonging is core to how we work, who we select, and how we develop—an expectation inherent in every decision we make.

Belonging and creating unique spaces for everyone is our business—it is understood and accepted by each employee, intern, and external partner. We go to extraordinary and expensive lengths to vigorously infuse and religiously protect these values and expected behaviors.

We put these together in our bible, which we call "Our Way: A Beautiful Mess." This tells our story, articulates our identity, and keeps us connected. We use "Our Way" for everything in our company—even the most challenging conversations. We make things not about the individual but rather the expectations we share. This process has been transformational. When we are true to this bible, we are most authentically ourselves, and we can make the most difficult decisions easier and less personal by removing anything about the individual and making it about our shared agreement. "Our Way" has even given me the strength and authority to ask family members not to be part of the company because they don't fit a given part of our values and behaviors—difficult, but necessary. This commitment to each other is core to our daily interactions.

One of my favorite messages to leaders is that you have one choice: Change the people or change the people. That is it. Change the people by giving them defined expectations and letting them live up to them. Or change them out because they cannot meet your standards. This places the onus on them—not you. I always say that rarely do leaders fire employees; more often, employees fire themselves. Again, when the identity is clearly articulated and lived, not just in posters on walls and "About Us" pages on websites, people will have all they need to decide whether they fit.

WHAT HAPPENS WHEN WE LOSE OUR CULTURAL IDENTITY

Most who meet me would never guess that I was once a part of "The Greatest Show on Earth." In many ways, there is no greater metaphor for belonging than the circus. The ecosystem there creates belonging for a group of people who most would consider outsiders. Throughout the ages, the circus has accepted people who have had labels projected onto them. Freaks. Misfits. Daredevils. Carnies. And many other labels associated with the circus. But, in its daily operation, the circus has been a group who came together, worked together, and lived and traveled together in its own reality while presenting mystery, wonder, beauty, and even death-defying feats under the big top. Performers embraced their uniqueness through their individual abilities while having pride in the whole of the show. And while working for Ringling Bros. and Barnum & Bailey Circus, I, too, found an inherent acceptance among us in being different—tall, short, bearded, animal trainer, plate spinner, tightrope walker—while also feeling special about being part of a larger tradition with a deep history in both America and the world. It truly was a global community of unique personalities from everyplace you could imagine but probably have never visited.

I had a firsthand view of the inner workings of Ringling Bros. as an old-fashioned promoter. You might think of it as an odd choice for a man of just twenty-two. But to me, it seemed like an adventure, and I immersed myself in it and learned what it meant to be part of a famous traveling show. We were, after all, showmen and -women. I was there at the beginning of the end of the circus and witnessed the early shifts the company faced—to give in and conform to changing times, or to give up what they authentically stood for. I was viciously threatened by animal-rights groups for things that quite simply were not true. I learned a lot about extremes during that time and what it meant to be on the other side of something, especially when the truth did not matter. Sadly, the identity of the circus, which had been carefully cultivated over a century and a half, failed to matter to its leaders when such an understanding was most needed—at the end of its existence.

As much as Ringling Bros. is a story of belonging, it is equally an American tragedy and lesson for leaders. After nearly 150 years in business, doing what they did best, they ended operations, vacating their place in its entertainment space. When faced with a changing environment and evolving societal norms, they chose the path that many leaders choose. They gave up what was central, enduring, and distinct about the organization, ultimately surrendering its identity rather than leveraging it to modernize and make changes that could also satisfy a contemporary appetite.

For 146 years, the circus was entertainment for all. But people didn't know (or perhaps care about) the extent to which the circus gave entertainers a place to freely practice and delight in their unique talents, how they cared for their animals, or the legendary business model they perfected to get people in the door to experience the circus and, more importantly, buy memorabilia and merchandise. The psychology of how they sold what they sold is as relevant today as any time in history. They appealed to the hearts and minds of people, especially children and their parents.

So many questions arise about why organizations suddenly fail after decades of success. Did they respond to the environment too fast or too late? Or should they never have responded? Each company has its own answer. But the big question remains: How do we allow American and/or global icons to disappear? Ringling Bros. was one such icon. It navigated the generations, circumventing challenges across nearly fifteen decades, somehow remaining relevant year after year—until it wasn't. Various explanations for its vulnerability have been offered:

- Ringling gave up its core values and became something different.
- No matter the advances or new innovations, it was still the circus that you only needed to see once.
- It was a lumbering icon that couldn't change quickly enough to keep up with the pace of technology and rapidly expanding entertainment access.
- It had simply been taken for granted that it would always be there, as it had been for the previous 146 years.

Perhaps this is less Ringling Bros. giving up or giving in and more a statement of the world we live in today. We have little tolerance for anything we don't understand. We gravitate to extreme and sexy headlines. We project stereotypes on things that we are reluctant to ever modify. We expose our youth more to what is ahead and much less to what is now or what was. This is precisely when identity becomes untethered and lost.

THE RESULT OF FORCED IDENTITY

Identity plays out in virtually every public organization, too. The question is, does the smaller organization—which could mean a subsidiary company or simply a division or department of a larger organization—take on the larger identity of the umbrella agency or institution, or form its own? Think about the U.S. military. Although every branch is part of the Department of Defense, each branch is unique. The Army, Air Force, Marines, Navy, Coast Guard, and Space Force all have specific identities borne of their missions, traditions, and history. Yet, even as new recruits are stripped of their old identities and given new roles and responsibilities fitting for the branch they joined, they all take an oath to defend the U.S. Constitution and obey the orders of the officers and the president as commander in chief.

In the next leadership exemplar, we explore the value of positioning identity over purpose for military leaders, as well as how the Belonging Rule translates when they transition into civilian occupations. Steve Johnson came to leadership first through West Point and later by earning an MBA from Rice University. Much of his understanding of identity came from his years of military service. Steve held leadership positions in the military all the way up through battalion command, where he led more than six hundred soldiers. Today he is the Long-Term Facility Strategic Project Manager for the Houston Texans. Steve told me that the character of a soldier emerges in how you see yourself and how others see you. In the military, you go through periods of shared hardship amid a culture of excellence. You are trained to believe that your unit is better than others. This identity of being exceptional can save your very life.

Yet Steve also talks about the tough but necessary balance military leaders must achieve. A leader must exercise judgment with high moral awareness. No soldier—or for that matter, leader—should feel superior to the people they are entrusted to protect. In the military, everyone is nested, down to the smallest unit. There is a hierarchy. You know that your actions specifically contribute to the whole of the operation. You can see and rely on the fit for every individual and every duty. And you know your own fit—it is literally drilled into you. You also know that if you don't perform, it impacts others. You are the person to fulfill that duty, to achieve the mission, to defend and protect, at all costs. As Steve describes it, soldiers are driven to perform the mission they are assigned. He reinforced that it doesn't matter "if everything goes to hell—if one person achieves the mission, then we all achieve." There is a collective spirit and support for the whole operation, not simply the individual, that forms a shared identity.

Thus, when you leave the military and resume a civilian identity, the transition can be a shock. You are thrust back into a life without that culture of each person fitting into a defined role, without a unit where everyone shares the same purpose, and without the overall structure the military provides. In Steve's case, his expertise and skill, honed by an incredible education in leadership, focuses on the operations and order of things. But his real talent is building leaders and establishing ecosystems where fit is recognizable and supported, where all can reliably depend on each other.

When Steve started working with the Texans, he noticed the daily operations that the team relied on needed to be streamlined to increase interactions across functions—even across functions (business, operations, and football) that had distinct identities as well. He instituted a complete redesign of all the spaces where the team spent time: the locker room, the equipment area, where they worked out—every aspect of their daily habitat. Although he compartmentalized areas by function, he also added elements such as glass walls, which allowed people to see all the activity and have that team feeling. He installed seating where players sat facing each other. Steve also increased the efficiency of the training facility via arranging it by primary functions: tape, treatment, and rehab. This intentional connectivity creates better flow. The locker room likewise fosters more interaction. The team began to enjoy being there, rather than feeling like they *had* to be there, and started to build camaraderie. In short, Steve nurtured belonging.

Steve thinks about belonging as *a feeling of pride, acceptance, shared purpose, and being part of a team with a clear identity.* It is what he works to create and support as a leader. He feels that the identity of a leader starts with character, competence, and commitment. These inform discretionary judgments, the decisions you make, and are all tied to professional practice. And Steve deeply believes that leadership comes from moral strength and the many aspects of your life that make up your identity.

Part of his work has also been with military healthcare. Steve shares that in a room full of military doctors, about half the room would identify as soldiers who are doctors and about half as doctors who are soldiers. I find this reassuring because it shows how your identity becomes complete the more you understand and accept all of what makes you, you. The purpose that we all share can be the same, but the individuals committed to that purpose bring in all that they are. We bond, we work together, we rely on each other, and we become a unit of individuals who have found our fit in shared identity.

Steve inspires me as I know he has inspired many others throughout his leadership journey. "Leadership is a privilege. It takes moral courage to be the supporting effort in a cause," he says, concluding that "part of leadership is at times realizing that you are not the main effort, you can be the supporting effort that creates a bridge that provides access for someone else." That to me is belonging leadership, wherever you serve and work.

Chapter 4

ARMING TODAY'S LEADER

Belonging Rule #4: **CHALLENGE EVERYTHING**

One of my favorite topics centers on the concept of challenging things in an age that recklessly disavows and discourages it. We have been taught to hold our tongues, hesitate when sharing our perspective, respect our elders, carefully weigh our words, and walk away from unpleasant conversations. We have been advised to avoid escalating difficult conversations at all costs. In other words, we have been silenced as leaders. Such silencing only makes sense in a 1950s world that hadn't yet met technology like the internet or cell phones. We live and lead in an environment in which information is always at everyone's fingertips. So why, then, should we accept the first answer we conceive, anything that pops up on our social media feed, or someone else's point of view as fact? Why has the critical ability to challenge boards, employees, leadership, constituents, bosses—even supposed facts—been taken away from us?

The ability to question and challenge is core to what it means to lead. In fact, of all the skills required for leaders, the ability to ask the right questions, challenge everything, and not give in to the compliant answer may top the list of importance. People have become experts at the fast response—the one they blurt out before you finish your statement or question. It is the answer we are expected to accept because the speed of the response and the confidence of the responder. By contrast, many leaders have become quiet for fear of being canceled or labeled argumentative and difficult by someone who is not fully informed or simply disagrees. Or worse, the leader has caught the eye of a social media troll that does not care about context, content, or anything other than taking down an easy target—you.

The lack of security that leaders at the top should feel is real and growing. It seems like it takes only one person or small team to derail a career of good. And, often in these cases, opinion is prioritized over fact. As a result, risk-averse organizational power structures choose the wrong solution. We expect leadership with purpose and a backbone, but instead many leaders hide behind the fear of erasure, ridicule by some extremist viewpoint inside or outside the company, political correctness, and anything else that masquerades as authority.

One wrong move. One poorly constructed post online. One old picture in an inappropriate pose or clothing or with the wrong people from decades ago. One mistake, honest or not, can serve as a death knell to a career, friendships, or your reputation. It is why people are more comfortable walking away. It is easier to accept whatever the answer is, even when the answer is not the full truth or the right response. We think we can wait and fix it later. And, perhaps we can, but at what cost to you, your company, or doing the right thing?

So, with all the societal traps and land mines seemingly surrounding leaders, many take the easy path. After all, the simpler solution presented to them was close enough. Yet, "close enough" or "good enough" are some of the most dangerous concepts in business. "Good enough" is a killer of people, ideas, and companies. Someone is working to pass you by—and at "good enough," there will always be someone shooting for something better. It is why settling when seeking answers is unacceptable. And it is why we must protect the need to challenge. With this in mind, **Belonging Rule #4 is Challenge Everything.**

Challenging also must be encouraged within leadership teams and healthy organizational cultures to the point where they cannot thrive without it. We cannot simply talk about challenge—not in these times. Instead, we must be active in our pursuit of it and practice the art of the question. This is not seeking conflict; as we will explore, that is a completely different concept. It is not about being argumentative. Nor is it about being difficult or expecting the impossible. It is, however, about expecting something better and, through the challenge, helping someone open new creative pathways in the brain through the act of change.

While I'm used to opening these pathways for others, it can be even more difficult—as I well know. Change was thrust upon me in the most unexpected way. I was looking for and needed someone to challenge me directly and in a way I hadn't yet experienced. That need was answered from an unlikely place.

I never thought in my life that I would be fired once, much less twice. But that is part of my story. After the founder of the marketing and advertising agency that I had worked at and led for over nine years died, his son, who was in finance and had no connection to the business, fired me. He did so after several weeks of meetings and strategy sessions where he talked about his vision of taking this very local company public. While working eighteen-plus hours a day week after week, I also found time to push back on the concept, the approach, and the overall thinking. In return, I was fired. I challenged everything and I lost. The irony is that I would have lost if I had stayed, too, as I would have been forced into a vision I could not actualize at a company where I could no longer lead.

Everything in my life was challenged. I had a wife, two children under the age of three, and a new dream home. My father, who I called for sympathy, said, "I'm so happy you were fired. You cannot have a life working until 2 AM every day. You are miserable to be around." He was right, but hard work was all I knew.

Then came the call that changed everything. Four days after I was fired, my phone rang. The conversation went something like this: "How dare you? How dare you walk out on me? Nobody is going to walk out on me." I was perplexed, as I hadn't walked out on anybody. I was fired and totally confused by this caller, whom I did not know.

I asked who this was. The person continued, "This is Priscilla, and I am the president of Texas Southern University. And I will be damned if the first person to walk out on me and my university is some skinny little white kid."

I responded that I was flattered—no one had referred to me as skinny in years. She continued, "My university will not be ignored, and you will work for us."

I asked, "Why me?" She explained, "Because I don't hire law firms, I hire lawyers. I want you."

But, I expressed, she didn't know me. Priscilla said, "I know that your old communication firm did great work, but it was *you* doing the work. I want you and will not accept any answer other than yes. Your choice is to start work next Wednesday as an employee or start work and I will be your first client."

Within a few days, I started my company and began working for TSU.

All I could think of was, wow! A "skinny little white kid" had just won his first client, a Historically Black University. Priscilla had challenged my beliefs on belonging and where I fit. How could a white guy like me, freshly fired and starting a brand-new company, be chosen to lead one of the university's most important and visible projects? Yet the president had seen something in me, something even I hadn't seen, and it wasn't color.

I learned more about acceptance in that moment than any time prior in my career. The president made it clear that it was her university and *my* university. She invited me in and made sure everyone knew I was not just part of the team, but a key player on it. Priscilla challenged her reports—and me—to understand how belonging starts with and comes from the leader.

PRIORITIZING THE CHALLENGE

We often hear that progress is motivated by inspiration or desperation. But in truth, there are many days, even years, when it is simply the routine work in front of us that consistently moves us ahead without the punctuation of big "aha!" moments. It is up to the leader to provide the inspiration and vision to enable others to see every moment with new wonder as an "aha!" By offering an effective challenge, a leader will be more equipped to create the capacity for the deep conversations and elevated thought that increase understanding and produce better outcomes. Navigating challenges is also a competency that leaders require to protect themselves as they expand in ways that create larger spaces for others to belong. Often, when challenge is approached as conflict, it pushes people away. At my firm, however, we rely on challenge as a method to bring people deeper inside and to spur a higher level of creativity.

The leader's commitment to challenge everything is critical, because once we accept that our abilities are always applied within a context that is going to change, we can learn to trust and rely on ourselves in a whole new way. Challenge encourages us to invite in and seek out what can be revealed that we did not see before. It allows us to vigorously advocate for diverse perspectives and elevate healthy discourse.

Traditional leadership values "knowing," but knowing is a temporary state. Many leaders and managers believe everything is knowable today, but that thinking is faulty, because what's not knowable is the future or humans' reaction to it. Knowledge can be whole in any given moment, but never complete. Leaders who claim to "know" and then rest there tend to become inflexible and even may be unconsciously fearful of learning something new. A better place to steady yourself as a leader is through knowing that you have access and input from a multitude of sources; that you can collaborate with and draw from many perspectives; and that you can trust yourself to use information, intuition, experience, and diverse input to actualize the best possible outcome. Since most of us naturally resist change, it is vital that you take a different mindset, believing instead that possibilities emerge within change and that the process of challenging can enhance this emergence as various options are considered, courted, and coaxed.

When you shift expertise to a kind of thinking rather than knowing, it can open you and your entire leadership team to more agility in getting from one state to another with greater trust and ease. The intentional leader uses all that is available to get to whatever or wherever is next, while thinking about the next, the next after the next, and the next after that. Great leadership requires you to continuously extend and challenge your thinking, your presence, your connection to your people, and your concept of the desired future state. Anticipation fed by greater understanding is the key to being prepared for what is possible, probable, or plausible. These words are closely related but require more examination when used in leadership contexts:

Possibility is about capacity; it can occur or be achieved; it presents opportunity for viability.

Probability is about what is likely to happen; all data and signs point in a direction, and without changing course, something is already in play.

Plausibility tells us something is reasonable to expect; that what is posited has merit.

When you consider the three, the arrival at greater understanding can set you on a completely different course of action that could mean time better spent or wasted. For instance, consider a leader with the choice of selecting a candidate who is a great fit and talent who stays for years, or one who only appears to fit because our need for their contribution keeps us from asking the deeper questions. Some leaders may possess the desire to challenge, but lack the nuance for the words and delivery. Others, no matter their approach, end up creating conflict that discourages the desired outcome. Still others are just uncomfortable with any form of challenge.

Regardless of where they begin, leaders can use an approach that actually invites people in and encourages not just the conversation but also the possibility of a different outcome and renewed creativity. This leadership tool, the Effective Challenge, was developed by Deutser to provide greater clarity and confidence as an alternative to the well-worn pro/con list that we're all so familiar with. Such lists often end up being a crutch that simply reveals what it is that we *want* to do versus what we *need* to do. That can be valuable, too, but an Effective Challenge is about exposing yourself to ideas and input that you might be overlooking. It invites and plays with difference in a way that surfaces new ideas, perspectives, and thought patterns.

THE CHALLENGE OF DEUTSER

People I work with expect me to challenge everything. It has become the way we do business in our company . . . and sometimes becomes a friction point when people believe they have exhausted every option after months of challenge, debate, and creation. I am most challenging when I believe there is something more creative just beyond us: a greater capacity for elegance, a latent idea or perspective that wants to appear. I'm sure it may seem that I always want more—and I do. I am unrelenting in my belief that more is attainable. More thought, more debate, more challenge—because with creativity there is no finish line. Likewise, there is no limit to what the human mind can create. One magnificent idea can give birth to multiple, even more magnificent concepts, if we allow it.

At Deutser, we use challenges in many ways. One of the ways we set up intentional challenges is by creating a ring of expectation. We hold people to agreed-upon behavioral expectations and expect our leaders and employees to effectively challenge one another if they go outside them. This is our social contract with each other, and it is documented in our organization's cultural guide—*The Deutser Way*. This is a literal printed book that explains who we are, where we're headed, and how we do what we do by explicitly stating our vision, values, and behaviors. We define what high, average, and low performance looks like for each behavior. Reliance on *The Deutser Way* allows us to challenge each other with a common understanding of what is expected, rather than looking at challenge as a personal attack. *The Deutser Way* creates a shared and balanced psychological contract, codifying what is often left unwritten and uniquely tethering employees to a common mission. It has saved many valuable employees who were going outside our agreed norms, and it pushed a few out—including family members—who couldn't withstand the challenge and modify their behavior. The more you challenge, the more you normalize expectations.

One of our unstated values—well, it is stated, but some don't like my choice of words—is "Show Your Underpants." Obviously, I don't mean this literally, but it is one of the most honest and open values we have. This value goes to the core of the concept that without being vulnerable, we can very rarely get to what we most need. As leaders, when we challenge, push, prod, and demand 100% of the truth, the tussle can feel uncomfortable (you'll learn more about how to do this effectively in chapter five). Soliciting challenges from others leaves us exposed, open for others to attack. But it is necessary. Vulnerability is central to having more faith and more confidence in your abilities and decisions. You learn to trust your efforts as much as you do your wins. Without vulnerability, you become risk averse, too afraid to try something new or different. Closing down like this also harms belonging because it becomes too easy to remain relegated to the sidelines. Vulnerability requires us to expose our truth to questions from others, to listen more deeply, and to remain keenly aware that we may have a biased view as we all reach to take part with larger capacity. To challenge effectively, we must dialogue, listen, and be willing to be wrong at times without losing faith in ourselves or each other.

What happens when you have a gut feeling that something isn't right, but you don't know what to say or how to get it closer to being right? The solution is in the question and in the way you challenge.

Challenging is necessary in a society that devalues listening and elevates the art of reaction. And challenging well is an art. Learning how to challenge effectively eliminates the tendency to avoid conflict. This process breaks down barriers and bridges rifts while creating an environment that fosters human connection. Ultimately, we're trying to find the right and best solution. The Effective Challenge is an intentional move from being adversarial or operating in fight mode and instead opening ourselves to a space of growth, possibility, and positivity. And, it's not personal.

CHALLENGE IS NOT CONFLICT

Let's clearly distinguish challenge and conflict. To some, they are one and the same. But they are not, and neither is the energy that surrounds both.

Conflict pits people or ideas against each other. Conflict has an inherent friction and rarely gets resolved without a loser and a winner. In the context of belonging, conflict is our enemy. Politics is rife with conflict: two sides constantly at odds positioning themselves for a win against the other side, assailing each other with vitriol while resisting any workable solution. This is no different from a family feud when two or more people disagree and fractures begin to deepen until the group splits into warring factions. Conflict creates a wedge and limits our willingness to pause, consider, find out more, and eventually gain understanding. Sometimes restoring that willingness takes one simple question; other times, it takes a months-long process.

Conflict is a circuit breaker that interrupts our leadership. When conflict escalates to a high intensity, it can completely drain our energy, distracting us from creative thinking and resolution. Such high levels of conflict inhibit our thinking and range of approaches. When leaders honestly evaluate the conflicts in all aspects of their lives—whether the source is the board, leadership, workforce, special groups, or even with friends or in their family—they begin to see how distracting and destructive these conflicts can be, even as they may have seemed only an annoyance.

Our aversion to conflict is why we teach the concept of challenging everything instead. Challenging must become a core skill for the agile leader who is looking to drive innovation, growth, and lead change. A creative spirit, an openness, and a sense of wonder and expectation accompanies the most effective challengers. Yes, there are times when challenge comes with brute force, but as with the power structures we discussed earlier, force is rarely the lasting solution. Force may even push us to make a challenge into a conflict—which we at Deutser work to avoid. More often, the challenge brings us to the middle, with cooperation and an ability to reduce any tension. It is a call for creativity and serves to to disarm the extremes. When met with excessive force or personal attacks, the effective challenger removes their energy, thanks someone for the attempt, and walks away. I use the metaphor of the spinning top. A top can only spin with energy that a person provides. When you stop feeding that energy, the top stops. So, too, does the unwarranted nastiness.

CHALLENGING THE WORKPLACE

When it comes to belonging, we cannot settle for the majority opinion or the first idea. If we do, we get stuck in our biased ways of thinking, revert toward sameness, and seek too many like-minded thinkers, while avoiding difficult but necessary challenging conversations. To create cultures of belonging, we should instead invite dissenting voices into dialogue and make sure we devote sufficient time, energy, and resources to challenging our own and others' ways of thinking.

It is time to challenge the way leaders lead, how workplaces are designed, the construct of interpersonal interactions across the organization, the titles and working structures of leaders and departments, the organizational alignment, and the invisible walls between departments in the same company. Opportunities to challenge abound in organizations because challenge is not about starting from a "terrible" place; rather, it is fundamentally an approach to continuously improve and learn from each other. Leaders can help accomplish this by creating people-supportive positions, such as establishing the post of chief belonging officer as an equal to the chief human resources officer, with both reporting to the CEO and working together as colleagues. What will be required is leadership who can set the expectation that this is a place where challenge makes us better, that there is common understanding that we challenge ideas, operations, and methodologies, not personal aspects of people. All it takes is an effective challenge from you, the leader. Later in this chapter, I'll show you how the concept of "let go and add one" can increase belonging while boosting the bottom line.

Political Innovators Elevate Challenge over Conflict

Belonging touches every facet of our lives. It extends far beyond our personal and professional actions and standing. When we think about the things that divide and label us and create the greatest angst, politics tops every list. We may challenge the conflict-laden political system with our friends and family, but little ever gets done to drive the necessary change most people want to experience.

This is why I became fascinated with an innovative political group that was built on the principle of driving change through effective challenge. My goal with this discussion is not to promote one organization or ideology but rather to show what challenge looks like in different places, politics included.

In 2009, Nancy Jacobson founded a centrist, nonpartisan political organization aptly named No Labels. This group works to bring people together—interestingly, even people at the far edges of both political parties—who are no longer satisfied with the deep partisan divide in our country. No Labels is working to find a better way to navigate challenging and contentious issues. The organization began with the belief that both the extreme left and right have well-developed voices that nobody in the center has been able to establish. Yes, there are the few exceptions where people "cross the aisle," but No Labels's call to action is for political realignment where the middle can be heard and organized.

No Labels is designed to promote societal and political change through discourse. It creates opportunities for people to come together to listen, learn, and understand. No Labels works to involve people in solutions, and leaders of the organization identify the Belonging Rules as part of their constructive pathway forward.

In our conversation with Nancy Jacobson she describes the organization's work as starting to build the allies inside. People who believe in a new way. No Labels became matchmakers of putting them together, which Nancy explained to us, "When you put legislators together, they want to legislate. One action came from a simple observation that to legislate, your bills must pass from the House to the Senate, but they would go nowhere. Our best innovation was matchmaking senators with representatives in Congress. We created the relationships and people found each other. This work focused on identifying and then matching representatives from each party who were in the middle, yet still divided by party. This opened dialogue between two individuals tasked with solving problems. In fact, the group first called these pairings Problem Solvers."

Over the past decade, extremes grew louder and deeper. Ryan Clancy, chief strategist of No Labels, described to us how belonging influences people interested in the political middle this way: "Oftentimes we talk in a language that is a little clinical and cold. We talk about being pragmatic and problem solving. Part of the reason we're starting to break through is this emotional appeal that there are these two powerful negative forces in each extreme that are increasingly chasing people to the middle. Someone looks over there and says, 'I can't go there, those people are crazy' and then they look over this other way and say, 'Those people are crazy too.' And they end up in this middle and find others there, from both political parties and with independents in this middle space and they say, 'These are my people.' Their first sense of belonging here is that they don't belong in the other places. By default, this becomes the place for them. The right and the left have such a structural advantage because they get to just hit the fear button over and over. Along with the messaging of "Give us money." We're not trying to appeal to people that way. People are rightly skeptical. There are many people, though, who want to believe and want to trust that this could all come together." And, I might add, come together in the middle.

Driving people in the center includes the realization that they have more in common with their mirror-center from the other party than they do with the extremes of their side. No one thought that you could motivate this group and get enough action to make a sustainable difference. Yet No Labels has been working in this space, bringing to life a vision for a different kind of cooperation than that currently experienced between deeply divided party lines.

Founder Nancy Jacobson tells us, "We don't have a dark view. We truly believe that if you bring these people together and create an environment where they feel respected, where they feel valued, their opinion matters. And nobody allows that in our Congress."

I am confident that this is true, and I remain excited for continued progress and ability to bring people together to create dialogue, inspire change, and challenge effectively when so much is at stake—the future of our country.

This is a group that understands that politics is built on conflict. If politicians can sustain that conflict, then they often stay in power with their established power structures in place. However, when we shift the paradigm from conflict to challenge and encourage listening without labels, we fundamentally change the spirit, the dialogue, and the result. This is not about moving people from one side to the other or challenging their identity; it is about using the Belonging Rules to fix a broken system that doesn't work for anyone in the middle.

THE MENTAL CHALLENGE

When we think about challenging, we often jump toward challenging others' perspectives and think about challenge as a form of confrontation. What if instead we stopped to think about the benefits of challenging as a uniquely beneficial form of inquiry, one that could enhance our brain health while helping us create stronger bonds with diverse groups? In my company's work with Dr. David Eagleman, a neuroscientist, best-selling author, and science communicator at Stanford University, we have begun to dig deeper into the power of the brain and how it is wired and needs challenge.

Questioning, seeking out novel experiences, and attempting to learn new things all keep the brain agile. Dr. Eagleman has partnered with Deutser on some of our most innovative performance programs targeting the brain and safety. In our collaborations, we work to understand how the brain allows bias, mind traps, and weak signals to influence action or inaction and how challenge helps overcome these potentially dangerous concepts. Unaddressed bias, mind traps, and weak signals contribute to decreased performance and situational awareness as well as increased mistakes in repetitive work. It also contributes to accidents.

When people challenge their brains, through asking themselves questions or trying new experiences, they are able to overcome the bias and mind traps and become more attuned to the weak signals around us. The point of our challenge work with the brain is to focus not only on the necessary challenge that is required within the workplace, but the internal, personal challenge that is required for improved individual performance as well.

This challenge is not only important, but it is necessary from a health perspective as well. As we age, there are powerful and potent effects of challenging on brain health. Neuroscience research on plasticity suggests that our brains degenerate as we age, but that learning new things helps us avoid cognitive decline. If we are always looking for ways to improve and actively searching out new challenges that are frustrating but achievable, that's a beginning step to keeping a healthy brain. The level of challenge forces the brain to take on new information. Just like the adage "we are what we eat," we also are what we learn. Eagleman says, "The truth is that we are what we put into our brains. That's what makes us who we are, because of brain plasticity." Thus, it's important to think about what we are putting into our brains. There is a difference between consuming TikTok and something that is going to challenge the brain and increase learning. It is why we offer the challenge to clients to provide information, content, and even book clubs to stretch their employees' brains, even when they are not at work. Yes, it is optional, but at the same time, it provides an opportunity for continued growth, learning, and increased brain plasticity. Most leaders aren't focused on the brain, yet it offers a benefit to the employee as well as the company when allowed.

Challenging Confined Thinking

We are often taught through lecture, by someone in a position of power telling us what to believe, what's real, what's true. As we grow up, we're socially conditioned that it's inappropriate to ask too many questions. Comments like "that's just the way it is" or "because I said so" teach polite and well-behaved children to believe that the way the world works is to not question things. Instead of looking at all facets of life as mysteries, as hypotheses deserving a scientific test and experimental approach, we go along with what is, especially in our educational system—and almost always to our own detriment. Eagleman argues that "the more that we shake up the circuits by challenging the brain, doing new things and expanding our abilities, the more that new pathways form. We can see things in fresh ways as opposed to simply running through the routines." This is fundamental in today's ever-changing environment. Things around us are evolving and we, too, must keep our brains pliable and open for change. It is an important practice.

Questioning the world around us is a gift. As humans, we have the unique ability to ponder, reflect, ruminate, and ask questions of ourselves and one another. Sometimes, what stands in our way is ourselves. In our work with Eagleman, he reminds our clients and their leaders, "The key is that your brain always wants to say, 'I've got it. I've got a complete internal model of the world now." But we must keep challenging to keep growing, to stay sharp and expand our understanding of the context within which we live. Ours is a society where people pay us to act like we know everything—especially the leader. What if we turned this model on its head and instead asked each other more questions? Our lack of questioning creates stagnation, and this stagnation is incredibly palpable in business environments. It may be counterintuitive: when we challenge, we think we're working against something, but instead we are creating capacity for insight and innovation.

Questioning, challenging, and the desire to learn have implications for belonging and organizational effectiveness as well. In his book, *The Art of Asking,* Terry Fadem of Wharton's Institute for Innovation Management argues that asking better questions can shape the future of your organization. In hundreds of surveys and interviews with organizational leaders, Fadem observed that managers tend to get into interrogation ruts, asking the same questions repeatedly, because these questions fall within their comfort zone. Fadem suggests that managers begin with "What if . . ." to allow more options to come to light and for creative thinking and innovative solutions.

The ability to embrace questioning and discomfort is also at the heart of inclusive leadership. People often prefer the comfort of sameness because the brain favors habituation, where it can go on autopilot through routine. When thinking about inclusive leadership, we must train our brains to actively engage with difference rather than running from it. Leaders agile in creating belonging approach their work from a place of humility, prioritizing the desire to connect people from diverse backgrounds in a context where communication can allow them to safely and effectively challenge issues that many of us don't feel completely sure about. Inclusive leaders are always learning, and that's why they are so important for organizational effectiveness. Research from BetterUp finds that teams with highly inclusive leaders demonstrate 150% higher belonging, 140% higher perceived organizational support, 90% higher team innovation, 50% higher team performance, 140% higher team engagement, and 54% lower turnover intentions. Effective challenge gives process to inclusive leadership. Inclusive leaders must be consistently willing to challenge their own beliefs, to listen from a place of wanting to learn and understand, and to remain open to new insights and ways of thinking.

This is not simply the practice of inclusive leaders. It is also part of the brilliance of some of the most renowned artists and inventors. These greats actively worked to remain open to new ideas and make space for challenge, which in turn influenced the creation of some of the most important art and inventions.

In conversations with Eagleman, he challenges us to never confine ourselves by thinking there's a single answer to things and to never settle for the first idea. In many ways, his research and thinking on this are one of the great influences of our company and how we approach developing the most innovative and original solutions—never allowing the first idea to prevail without challenge. Eagleman shared vivid examples of how famous artists like Monet and inventors like Edison went about this in their own work, illustrating, "This is why Monet painted over thirty views of the Rouen Cathedral in different lighting. It's that he didn't take his first answer. He kept challenging himself over and over to really understand what he was seeing. Hokusai painted over thirty views of Mount Fuji in Japan. It's not that he thought he'd done something wrong or wasn't satisfied with what he'd done, but he wanted to be able to see things in fresh ways to really operate in the moment . . . Picasso painted fifty-seven variations of this painting *Las Meninas* by Velázquez, because he kept going back and digging deeper. And by the way, Thomas Edison implemented something in his laboratories that I copied from him, and I implemented my lab, which is this idea of idea quotas. So, whenever somebody would come to him and say, 'Hey, I'm stuck on this,' he'd say, 'Great. I want you to come back next week with five ideas about how to solve this.'" What they all knew was the first idea will almost always follow the path of least resistance. It is why the challenge is so crucial. And, when you are asking for four more ideas, it can be draining and demoralizing. But, it is necessary to create an environment like Eagleman describes where we can "allow this creativity to blossom and allow us all to be operating in the present rather than just operating like automata through some sort of checklist." And all it takes is an understanding that the brain relies on challenge.

THE EFFECTIVE CHALLENGE

When done right, challenge is never personal. Effective challenge is not about attacking the individual. It is always about the work, the issue, or the desired future state. Our goal is to make the conversation neutral. The art of the challenge is where the greatest and most creative outcomes are birthed. When we challenge, we are looking for that next-level creative thinking and solution. This can be uncomfortable, as most things are when we work with others in challenging spaces. But arriving at the right solution is too important not to use challenge. Likewise, our brains naturally want us to choose the path of least resistance. But we must be willing to push ourselves to question and challenge everything around us. Living in the status quo leaves us waiting for the inevitable change to happen around us. Challenge keeps us relevant, creative, and in the conversation.

So, what becomes more important than the challenge is the practice of the challenge. How we approach challenge is everything—it either invites people in, creating new possibilities and potential, or it pushes them away and provokes conflict. To guide people toward invitation, we have developed the Effective Challenge: ten steps to facilitate a healthy discussion and yield a more positive outcome. Each step starts with of one of the letters C-H-A-L-L-E-N-G-E.

C—Change the mind. Tell yourself and your team that you already have the right answer, and you have a duty to question it anyway.

H—Have empathy. Ask yourself, "What is the other person thinking/feeling/expecting?"

A—Align outcomes. What is our desired future state? What are we trying to do here?

L—Lean into the direction. How does our existing solution get you to the desired future state?

L—Let go and add one. Let go of your attachment to what is proposed. What is one thing we can do to improve the solution?

E—Everything goes. What would change if we could approach the solution in a totally different way?

N—Negotiate a pathway. Ask yourself and your team, "Where do we go from here? Of our collective thoughts and choices, which elements move us in the most desirable direction?"

G—Get honest. Was anything left unsaid, and did I share 100% of my truth?

E—Encourage agreement. Work collaboratively. Agree on the direction together.

And the final step is the endorsement that we again got it right. "Pierce it with Positivity!" Finish strong by saying out loud, "This solution is the right one and is the best pathway to achieve our desired future state."

The ability to defuse any conflict gives us the chance to channel that energy into more creative uses—to connect on solutions rather than continue in opposition, which blocks energy and ideas. Acknowledging that you have an acceptable solution adds cohesion and unity in working together toward that solution. Through this method, you take pressure off yourself to come up with the perfect answer and release everyone from having to "be right."

Each step in the Effective Challenge allows you to dissect important elements of the conundrum at hand. But sometimes we don't want to use all the steps. In those circumstances, we use the mini challenge, which is only three steps long:

1. Acknowledge that you already have the right solution.
2. Let go and add one: Give up your attachment to the original solution. Then add one new thought, changing or questioning what already exists. The power of simply adding or changing one thing, no matter how small or large, is transformational. This is the most freeing and often most creative step.
3. Encourage agreement: Agree on *the* one change. What single change takes our original solution to the next level, and how will we revise our original solution so it's the *best* solution?

EFFECTIVE CHALLENGE

Challenging well is an art. In a society that values reaction over listening, challenging well has never been more vital.

What do you do when you have a gut feeling that something isn't right, but you don't know how to fix it? Have you ever been in a situation when you know something is off, but can't find the best path toward a better solution?

Rather than creating conflict, or avoiding conflict altogether, use the below guide to learn the steps to challenge well. At the end of the day, we're trying to get the right and best solution. It's not personal.

EFFECTIVE CHALLENGE STEPS:

C **hange the mind.** Tell yourself it's right and that you have a duty to question it anyway.

H **ave empathy.** What is the other person thinking/feeling/expecting?

A **lign outcomes.** What is our desired future state? What are we trying to do here?

L **ean into the direction.** How does our solution get us to our desired future state?

L **et go and add one.** Let go of the attachment to the solution and add a positive change.

E **verything goes.** How could we approach the solution in a totally different way?

N **egotiate a pathway.** Where do we go from here?

G **et honest.** Was anything left unsaid, and did I share 100% of my truth?

E **ncourage agreement.** How can we agree on the direction together?

Pierce it with Positivity!

Repeat this statement out loud. This solution is the right and best solution to achieve our desired future state.

In this exercise, you will reflect on two unique scenarios and run through the effective challenge framework to help you rethink (a) a past decision and (b) an important future decision. You can run through this exercise individually or share it with your work team/broader organization. The framework is meant to spur debate and discourse, opening people up to the art of challenging.

SCENARIO A

What is an important decision you recently made?

_____

How did you make that decision?

_____

Go through the Effective Challenge steps for that decision. Write below:

C **hange the mind.** It's right and I have a duty to question it anyway.

_____

H **ave empathy.** What is the other person thinking/feeling/expecting?

_____

A **lign outcomes.** What is our desired future state? What are we trying to do here?

_____

L **ean into the direction.** How does our solution get us to our desired future state?

_____

L **et go and add one.** Let go of the attachment to the solution and add a positive change.

_____

E **verything goes.** How could we approach the solution in a totally different way?

_____

N **egotiate a pathway.** Where do we go from here?

_____

G **et honest.** Was anything left unsaid and did I share 100% of my truth?

_____

E **ncourage agreement.** How can we agree on the direction together?

_____

Pierce it with Positivity!

Repeat this statement out loud. This solution is the right and best solution to achieve our desired future state.

SCENARIO B

What is an important decision you need to make in the future?

_____

Write down one of the options you are considering for that decision:

_____

Go through the Effective Challenge steps for that option:

C **hange the mind.** It's right and I have a duty to question it anyway.

_____

H **ave empathy.** What is the other person thinking/feeling/expecting?

_____

A **lign outcomes.** What is our desired future state? What are we trying to do here?

_____

L **ean into the direction.** How does our solution get us to our desired future state?

_____

L **et go and add one.** Let go of the attachment to the solution and add a positive change.

_____

E **verything goes.** How could we approach the solution in a totally different way?

_____

N **egotiate a pathway.** Where do we go from here?

_____

G **et honest.** Was anything left unsaid and did I share 100% of my truth?

_____

E **ncourage agreement.** How can we agree on the direction together?

_____

Repeat this statement out loud. This solution is the right and best solution to achieve our desired future state.

I embrace the challenge. I apply it in many different settings and find it useful for arriving at both simple solutions and the most complex. Here's an example. At an eclectic dinner party with a diverse group around the table, including clergy from multiple faiths, we began debating the idea of the challenge. The rabbi talked about the name "Israel" and how it translates to "wrestling with God." I became fascinated as he explained the name's meaning and the expectations surrounding it. He talked about the constant struggle of this classic conflict and how important gaining different perspectives is to his depth of faith. He described how two people can walk into a room with two perspectives and leave with three. His point was that challenge is embedded in his and other faiths and is an expected component of discourse on important topics. With that discipline, leaving with an informed, different perspective than where you started is a likely outcome.

This idea of mental sparring is why we have boxing bags and gloves in our Leadership Learning Labs, each adorned with graffiti that says, "Who's your sparring partner?" We want the challenge to be front and center as we teach leaders how to spar constructively on topics of importance. We teach the skill of challenge and help leaders convert it to an art form. Of course, there is no ring; we are simply teaching the art of the spar and necessity of challenging with our words.

We also use challenge in how we interview. We want people to like us, but we want them to know us from the first encounter. If you cannot withstand the multiple behavioral interviews , you will not excel in our company. We challenge candidates with our probing questions, our expectations, and our redirects and intentional interruptions. We don't want the practiced you—we want the real you. And we have developed a scientific approach to elicit the information we need. Our interviewees need to understand our culture of challenging everything.

We open workshops with a challenge as well. We ask leaders to fill out five oversized sticky notes by asking five open-ended questions, all starting with the word "why." It is the only time we accept the word "why" from leadership because, by its nature, it is divisive and confrontational. We ask leaders to challenge themselves and their colleagues with their questions. This is not about confrontation, but true challenge—and it is always done anonymously, to ensure the full impact and truth embedded in the question. When it comes to the Effective Challenge, the word "why" is a weapon to be used wisely, or never at all.

We also challenge how leaders see their organizations and their own leadership. Remember my earlier axiom that a leader has one choice: change the people or change the people. On the surface these options are the same. But leaders don't lead on the surface; they go deep. Leaders have the ability to create a framework for others to challenge themselves and create their own change. If they are unable to make the change, then leaders are challenged to change the people—as in, out of the organization. In either case, the challenge lies in the leader's ability to see the needed change and create the pathway. Sometimes it requires the simple add-one element; other times, a fundamental remake.

Some find my relentless desire to probe exhausting. Perhaps I would have been better off sticking with my law school endeavors. But I am not questioning to fluster; rather, to encourage. At times, the challenge evokes a raw, unvarnished response—sometimes tears or sheer anger. In either case, I am prepared to accept whatever my challenge elicits.

Today's leader must be armed with the tools that allow them to lead with courage. They must be committed to the truth and be willing to push people right to or just beyond their personal comfort line. We bring people into this state because we believe that they can contribute and create at a different level, even when it feels like the opposite to them. We believe that the brain has a misunderstood capacity and ability to fundamentally explore and push boundaries. Tapping this capacity is why we do what we do and why we expect so much more from our people. We believe they can get to a higher state with more creative output. When we allow the effective challenge to do its best work, reaching that higher state comes naturally.

LEADERS WHO CHALLENGE

Early in his career, Blair Garrou, co-founder and managing director of Mercury Fund, had become known for successfully replicating the Silicon Valley playbook in Middle American cities by helping to create viable startup technology ecosystems there. Supply and demand had left an imbalance of capital available for funding technology startups, and Blair was looking to build the next generation of great deals outside of both Wall Street and Silicon Valley. For over a decade, Mercury focused on the underrepresented entrepreneur, in this case a startup founder without access to capital. However, over time, Blair found that the traditional playbook had left massive demographics behind without access to capital and resources. He wanted to create belonging and access for black, Hispanic, and female entrepreneurs who previously had been dismissed as "undesired and underserved" for venture capital. Mercury believed that there were incredible investments to be made in these founders, but it would take real inclusive work at both the fund and the community level to execute, so they began to build relationships with organizations who worked with historically underserved startup founders.

Over the next few years, by all measures, the firm was wildly successful. But that didn't stop the phone call Blair made to Deutser, not only to question but to challenge everything in his business.

The call came on a dreary Sunday afternoon as COVID-19 was challenging many of Mercury's entrepreneurial companies and bearing down Blair's spirit. He questioned whether to rebrand the entirety of his company or rethink it altogether. He challenged the future and his ability to more meaningfully serve the communities he so dearly wanted to reach.

We came in to consult and challenged every facet of his firm's existence to get the answers. He gathered partners and key shareholders from across the country for a painful but necessary examination. After days of reflective and at times contentious conversation, it was Blair's deeply personal challenge of the potential value of inclusiveness that changed the discussion and the future of the company.

Not allowing the simple, obligatory discussion of DEI to suffice, we forced leadership to give meaning to each value and prove it. We shot down every definition they offered and challenged every word, in order to debate whether they were living by these words and committed to the work they represented. We recognized that the answer to this inquiry would change not only how they worked internally but also who they would fund and how they could redefine their reach into the industry.

As a result, Mercury Fund redesigned the core of its business to add materially improving historically overlooked entrepreneurial communities to their offerings. Further, the firm reimagined its values to include entrepreneurial passion, intellectual curiosity, intentional integrity, an innovation mindset, and being intrinsically inclusive. The moment the leaders arrived at their values, especially "intrinsically inclusive," the rebirth began. They concluded that the overused idea of "inclusiveness" had no tangible value, but the concept of being "intrinsically inclusive," if executed true to their mission, would be a game changer. They were right.

Upon this realization, Blair jumped out of his seat, pulled his protective COVID mask down, and implored his team to understand that these values were not just words, but a fundamental way to run the business and forever differentiate their offerings. After pausing, he said, "It is also how we demonstrate what it means to do right and change people's lives." This moment moved the leaders to join in and build a future around what it meant to truly be intrinsically inclusive. It was the catalyst to diversify the leadership and investment teams; rethink the ecosystem around community building; and firmly plant a commitment to mentoring and enabling by providing resources, training, and support to a new community of entrepreneurship.

The result was surprising. It became clear that their future wasn't about rebranding or opening or closing funds. Rather, the way forward was to realize their shared vision and reimagine the future of the business and its potential impact on the industry as a whole. It was in this exploration that they began to see how they could fundamentally differentiate from others in the venture capital space by infusing their values into their operations, which reinvigorated both their business and those of other entrepreneurs, who now had doors of opportunity opened for them.

Now, just a few short years later, Mercury is the gold standard for its work in underserved communities. It has funded many more underestimated entrepreneurs, most if not all of whom had been rejected or rebuffed by other firms. In addition to those they funded, Mercury developed programs for budding entrepreneurs and their efforts in underserved communities, knowing that most of them would not meet their funding criteria. Yet to Mercury, it did not matter who fit and who did not. They knew, as part of their vision and desire to create this new ecosystem of support for budding entrepreneurs, that Mercury had an inherent obligation to fund development and growth, even if they would not ultimately fund the ventures themselves.

Mercury kept doubling down on living their commitment. They started using their space and resources to host events for female founders and founders of color. They kept breaking down the walls in venture capital, teaching the participants at every step how to do it. The impact has been significant, as many of these leaders have participated in workshops and personal development they never could have afforded or accessed. Further, it helped to connect them with each other and begin to build the pioneering ecosystem at the heart of Mercury's vision. Mercury has produced manifold returns for their investors.

Blair explains that the values they adopted allowed all to come together and have one voice. Of his team, he says, "There is high performance because everyone is doing the best work of their careers." Blair told us that Mercury Fund was named partly in tribute to America's program to put an astronaut in orbit around the time of JFK's famous speech: "We choose to go to the moon in this decade and do the other things, not because they are easy, but because they are hard." Referring again to his team and their boundaries, Blair reminds us, "We live as humans to find a sense of purpose in community. You can't have community without feeling like you belong. Community means you participate. Everyone has a voice, and everyone participates and feels like they have agency."

When we prevent ourselves from favoring sameness and living in echo chambers and truly seek to challenge our thinking, we unlock a hidden creativity that empowers us to shoot for the moon. And, when we do, we create unmistakable blueprints for how to keep challenging in our newfound spaces of belonging.

Chapter 5

LEADING THE MOVEABLE MIDDLE

Belonging Rule #5: **DEMAND 100% OF THE TRUTH**

Now more than ever, the truth is being challenged. What happened to it? Why the need to create a Belonging Rule to address what should be fundamental to us all? It is harder and harder to believe, much less accept, the truth because we've lost our confidence in recognizing what is true. We live in a time where we have our own truths and understandings and continuously see that there is no collective truth, only what is shoved to the far edges, vigorously defended by some and rejected by others. This dynamic sets up an unhealthy tension and resistance that results in little give-and-take. And some choose to remain silent and not challenge alternative views—thus deepening the divide. This is destructive for everyone. When we don't demand the truth, it fuels an environment that lacks trust, understanding, empathy, and belonging.

For too long we've left the extremes to their own opinions and devices. They have applied their versions of the truth and inserted them into our businesses. The lines have become blurred, and the truth has been expanded to fit a particular viewpoint that serves some but not most. Leaders have allowed others—inside and outside their organizations—to not only define the conversation but also redefine what is and is not true. This is compromising our businesses, our future, and the workforce and constituents that can be overlooked yet are crucial to driving performance—from the middle. Thus, it becomes the imperative of the leader to not only lead with the truth but also demand the truth. No longer can the leader allow the extreme views or the nuanced perspectives to dominate the conversation or manipulate the truth. There is a confidence and commitment from the leader to lead with the full truth—and if it is not known, have the conviction to seek it out. What leaders decide to do or not do in the moment determines not only their fate but that of their company—and, more importantly (if often as a lower priority), the fate of their people.

At the edges of belonging is a focus on fitting in. That fit may be with an extreme of like-mindedness or in the middle within a more diverse set of viewpoints and perspectives. There is a measure of truth for the extreme position—and it is fiercely shared, causing deep belonging. And there is perhaps a greater truth in the middle, where different views are accepted and challenged. The fit in the middle is created by the acceptance of difference.

Meeting expectations without giving in or giving up what we believe simply to fit in creates tension that threatens belonging. The decisions we make in meeting those expectations are complicated by the information we find or input we are given. So much of the data we acquire comes from the loudest or most extreme perspectives, and while there may be truth in them, they don't always tell the full truth. Rather, they are narratives, designed to persuade for a particular purpose. As if recognizing this danger, Oxford Dictionaries chose "post-truth" as its 2016 Word of the Year, explaining the concept as "relating to or denoting circumstances in which objective facts are less influential in shaping public opinion than appeals to emotion and personal belief."

Beyond being just a business problem, this pull toward extremes and assault on truth is a growing societal problem, too. Michelle

Bachelet, former United Nations high commissioner for human rights, suggests that because we have so much information at our fingertips, we tend to be led astray by disinformation. It's so easy for various groups to manipulate a narrative or swing people to an extreme perspective without their seeing the underlying algorithms that drive that information. She says this leads to "false impressions of broad popular support for or against certain ideas."

We experience such false impressions daily through multiple channels: news outlets with outlandish views peddled as mainstream and truthful; nameless, faceless social media voices pushing perspectives as facts; anonymous missives presenting a point of view as the majority opinion with such authority that few question its minority perspective; and disengaged groups who quietly undermine things in their own organizations by creating a wedge in their belief systems. No wonder we sometimes focus on the loudest voices and have our attention grabbed by the fringes in our companies and society. The people and groups that live there are dangerous, not because of the harm they can do, but because of what we ignore when our attention moves from the middle to focus on the extremes. We are foolish to think we have the power to change them. What we *can* change is the middle—the people on whom you rely, and often overlook every day, simply because they are doing their job. Leaders misplace their effort, time, and resources when focusing on the fringes at the expense of the middle.

Belonging relies on engaging and gaining commitment from those in the middle. People there often feel left out and underappreciated. Their talents go untapped, their contributions are rarely recognized, and their potential is underestimated. Yet leaders' attention is rarely captured by this agile audience—after all, they are quiet, willing, and consistently the steady force doing necessary work. Fortunately, leaders can change their approach and use what I call the moveable middle to their advantage. And all it requires is the truth—the full truth, even if it is untimely or uncomfortable. This brings us to **Belonging Rule #5: Demand 100% of the truth**.

I think about the middle as moveable because historically it has been characterized by groups that are willing to evolve, change, and grow with you and your needs. They have already bought in and are the center of your organization's sense of belonging. They are not loud or demanding, but they have needs, starting with being given 100% of the truth. They want information—not corporate mumbo-jumbo, but facts. Give them what they need and trust them to take action and make the right decisions. Over and over, they will prove you right.

The real solution to most problems lies in the middle and how they belong. However, the middle is often where the tension quietly resides, simmering below the surface due to office politics or lack of psychological safety that prevents people from navigating toward the truth through clear, consistent dialogue. The middle is also where leaders are likely to find the quietly disenfranchised and disconnected, those who want no part of any extreme and only want to keep their job. Leaders who avoid the truth mistakenly underestimate the power of the middle. The energy and conflict kicked up by people at the extremes steals precious time and attention, keeps people focused on a single distracting issue, and makes sharing ideas or engaging in productive debate feel unsafe. Progress and innovation stall and employee happiness and retention dwindle.

A FOREIGN CONCEPT

Truth begins when people become clear on who they are, what they do, and how they do it. One of the great values of truth is that it creates an opening that reveals complexities and offers breathing room. As leaders, we're conditioned to solve problems by meeting energy with more energy. The result is that we invest tremendous resources in addressing the extremes. But in every extreme, even those of talent and innovation—including the things that seem to drive what we most want—it can be easy to get caught up by the velocity and momentum.

The effort of attending to the best and worst of what is happening opens a chasm between what is most immediate and seems urgent, and what makes up a whole truth where all is considered, people are included, and the work is cooperative. We express 100% of the truth when we lay everything out on the table and begin the real work.

It sounds easy. And it should be. But 100% of the truth is a foreign concept in a world that shuns and disincentivizes it. We have been conditioned to live with and lead with whatever truth is convenient and at whatever level of truth we feel comfortable with—even if it is not even close to 100% of it.

It isn't always apparent how truth will serve us, but truth is the ultimate servant that allows us to step into any contentious or overlooked space with confidence and clarity. It is ultimately our great protector—maybe not in the moment, but long term. It is fundamental not only to creating belonging but also sustaining it. Consider a conversation or a relationship; when we learn that the full truth has not been part of the equation, we can feel left out. Relatedly, when we lead with less than the complete truth, we leave ourselves open to being exposed through what we have omitted.

CHALLENGING THE TRUTH

As a facilitator to belonging, truth allows us to know where we all stand—and where we all fit. It enables us to let go of "reserving" something in case we need it to better position ourselves if we're being cheated or exploited. That doesn't release us from relying on wisdom or permit us to enter a state of suspended naiveté or magical thinking. Instead, truth brings clarity to where we stand at any given moment, in the whole of what we are all facing, with more clarity about what we should engage. Truth brings those who have checked out back in—and forces those who use their version of the truth as power to be pushed out.

Here's the secret to truth: when you enter a space for truthfulness, every truth combines with yours, further clarifying the picture. Imagine a fuzzy image that becomes clearer with each truth added until the image is crystal clear. To ensure our shared images come out clear, we need everyone to share their truth. Too often, however, we allow ourselves and others to withhold the truth.

Our consulting work challenges the truth. It forces leaders and leadership teams to delve deeply into the uncomfortable—which is the full truth. Most companies, even high-functioning, high-performing ones, operate in the comfortable area of 75% to 80% of the truth. Think about what discussions they are missing. What disagreements are being shelved. What issues are being covered up. At Deutser, we see the most complex and complicated issues living in this remaining percentage. It is often the place of the most contentious disagreement. Yet, it is also the area of disagreement that eliminates conversation and instead furthers a façade of agreement on all the other "important" issues. We best serve the middle when we demand 100% of the truth all of the time. By merely wishing and hoping our omissions don't impact them or expose the shortcomings of our leadership teams, we leave that middle exposed and vulnerable.

Oftentimes the full truth is hard, especially within tight-knit families and organizations where the relationships are more personal. It can be biting—even divisive. But, in our work, we have found that the hard truth is most necessary in groups that are the tightest and share more personal bonds. We see the truth as a connector between multigenerational families and organizations, where people have fallen into in a "go along to get along" mindset and sugarcoat or gloss over anything that feels uncomfortable or acrimonious. The leader of these groups must initiate a conversation around 100% truth, even if it is with a nonthreatening question such as, "Have we thought about this from all perspectives?" Discourse is critical to creating a space for belonging, even amid disagreement.

BRIDGING A GENERATIONAL DIVIDE WITH 100% TRUTH

Kelly Zuniga is a seasoned leader operating in spaces of utmost importance. As CEO of Holocaust Museum Houston, she works tirelessly to lead a multigenerational effort to educate about the dangers of hate and prejudice across society. Her work has been challenged and, in some ways, compromised by other people's view of the truth—totally unsupported—and their desire to fundamentally change history. She battles daily against the extreme views and desire to change both the past and future based on manufactured perspectives. She actively works to preserve the truth for so many.

Her board and her leadership team faced a fierce generational divide over the vision for the museum's future and the growing national trends of Holocaust museums to consider linking with and expanding into broader-based human rights issues.

The founders of the museum, referred to as the first generation, are Holocaust survivors. Their effort and purpose have been to protect at all costs the full truth of what happened. Now, one might think this isn't necessary—that it is obvious. But it still shocks one to the core that anyone could possibly question if the Holocaust had even happened. I have been forever moved by my visits to former concentration camps, and have been changed by the relationship I established with a survivor who inspired me with his story of survival and his belief in a different future. Before he died several years ago, he charged me never to allow the truth to be manipulated or changed to fit someone else's story. It is part of the reason why I honor his memory.

Over the years, the museum quietly existed as a reminder of the Holocaust and a place where lessons about it could be learned. Faced with dwindling attendance, a shrinking philanthropic base, and an uncertain future because of broader interests, however, the museum was challenged to do what it had never envisioned—change with the times. This led to contentious dialogue and stiffening positions, all by people who cared passionately for the same cause and place. Basic conversations were misconstrued. Words were twisted and meanings changed by otherwise honest people who represented three generations, each of which shared different perspectives. Some were afraid to change, and others were afraid not to. Yet, at the core, they all cared about the survival of the place they all loved.

All parties needed to establish intergenerational trust, and the first generation particularly needed to accept the reality of passing the torch to those who had not personally witnessed the Holocaust's horror. The second generation grew up as descendants of the first-generation survivors. They expressed their passion for making sense of what had happened rather than solely preserving the memory, which they knew was core to their parents and grandparents. They wanted to protect and find meaning in their ancestral passage while keeping alive how this heritage impacted their families and people of their faith. Yet, there was also a third generation of participants to whom belonging is very important and who wanted to bridge the past of the Holocaust, applying context and meaning, by extending consideration to human rights of all kinds. These three generations of stakeholders needed to collaborate on a new vision for expanding the museum to position it for a changing future. Our pursuit of 100% truth (while also listening without labels) helped all three generations share their hopes, fears, and misconceptions, no matter how uncomfortable.

One complexity: the deep respect the second and third generations had for the survivors in the first unintentionally delayed needed changes to ensure the lessons of the past would never be forgotten. While the first generation seemed to propose a narrower interpretation of the museum's mission, the younger ones favored a more open approach, believing that they could accomplish what the survivors wanted and what the second generation believed the future required. They saw a need to be more relevant to other communities and to acknowledge other violations of human rights, especially those happening today. The younger generations wanted other communities to see that they also belong at the museum, that it offers so much relevance and understanding of how genocide affects our humanity—and that there is still so much that needs to be exposed and addressed.

All three generations were saying very similar things to each other without hearing each other. They spoke about protecting and preserving, but also about remaining relevant so that the museum would overcome the challenges of time and continue to operate in perpetuity. The process we implemented was designed to put forward the ideas and beliefs while removing the emotion. We stripped the vitriol and fear and replaced them with more clinical and basic human concepts. We allowed each generation to show what was at stake for the other generation. In this moment, the whole truth was the catalyst for understanding and change.

Through belonging-focused leadership and strong hearts, the old and young finally heard each other—or at least became willing to listen to the other side—by finding a way to connect the dots of history to current events of today. The ultimate result: strong agreement from all three generations based on the truth of genocide and human rights violations, and a reimagined, dramatically expanded and redesigned museum, bolstered by record philanthropic support that serves both the past and present as well as whatever is to come. All generations finally understood that their unwillingness to fully grasp and address their changing environment was jeopardizing both the past and the future they were so fiercely trying to protect.

One discovery that the process of increasing belonging through pursuit of 100% of the truth affords is the chance to always be mindful of what those around us are feeling at any given moment. The things people say may not be what they mean, but this doesn't necessarily indicate malicious intent. Many times, people say what they perceive you want to hear, don't want to let their guard down, or express shortened versions of the ideas they intend to convey. Likewise, you may be unaware of the deep hurt that what you believe to be reasonable comments, requests, or demands can trigger. When it comes to interpreting others' communications, one way to dive deeper into the full reality of what they're saying is by empathizing with the feelings and intentions beneath the veil of language they use. What is the mood in our pool of stakeholders? How is the news, the social climate, or the political landscape skewing the attitudes of the environment around us? A keen sense of the prevailing sentiment can give context to a perceived sensitivity. Making the effort to listen, uncover shared values, and join in areas where you can find early agreement that forms a foundation can help. Actively work to

- establish trust, acceptance of new ideas, and rapid change;
- bring out the leader in you and create a connective membrane that is flexible enough to adapt and permeable enough to admit a range of insight; and
- generate trust while leading with accessibility and accountability.

In our work with Kelly Zuniga she encourages all to "be the curator of speaking up. Take on speech that encourages hate. Expose how others can be negatively impacted and influenced by any kind of expressed hate. Be an advocate for positive change by learning more about what connects the past to the future." And that is what the museum is doing as a result of three generations understanding one another's truth. Holocaust Museum Houston is better able to educate about prejudice and hatred of all kinds, while also teaching about current atrocities and creating connections to make sure that the relevance and truth of the past is never sacrificed for an easier-to-digest, more palatable version of history.

Imagine trying to educate about the Holocaust after removing 20% of the story or the names of those murdered. That is 1.2 million people whose lives and stories would never have been preserved. Imagine telling any story from the past or present—slavery, genocides, discrimination of any group—and then discounting it by leaving out all the real information. This is how history then comes into question—when we tell only part of the truth, it is the only part that lives on. Worse, where there are holes in the story, they get filled with manipulated facts or misinformation. It is dangerous to us today and will remain so. Museums exist to preserve 100% of the truths of history—and to ensure stories of historical relevance remain accessible. Holocaust Museum Houston tells the story of the Holocaust, but it has successfully refocused to incorporate exhibits for understanding and conversation around diverse and sensitive topics. Today the museum is a gateway to understanding, speaking out, standing up, and creating a more unified, compassionate, truthful future.

After many months of working together to create belonging for all, the three generations of Holocaust Museum Houston contributed to a new vision statement for the museum that says so much:

> We envision a society that transforms ignorance into respect for human life, that remembers the Holocaust, and reaffirms an individual's responsibility for the collective actions of society.

As the museum opened its newly expanded facility and introduced its vision to welcome all generations, they did so with a simple but truthful messaging strategy built around one line: *It is hard to hate up close*. Those words capture the essence and spirit of the museum. They want to bring all people together and into the conversation. They want all to know that through education and truth, we can begin to eliminate prejudice and hate. They want people to see a basic human truth and ask all to get up close to things they have pushed away through bias, ignorance, or any other reason and finally see a different human connection as possible.

As leaders, we have a responsibility to seek the truth out, share it and encourage it in the spaces we occupy, and lean into discourse. We must fight for the truth, wherever we are. When we remove statues, change the truth, ban books, or force erasure of important historical events, no matter how painful or horrifying, we actively work against the truth. We can all work to ensure preservation of the truth individually and collectively, generation by generation.

THE PRESENCE OF TRUTH

The extreme voices are not always extreme; they may just be loud and passionate. At Holocaust Museum Houston, no side of the debate was engaging with malicious intent. But there was a thoughtful group in the middle that simply wanted to live up to the museum's mission. They wanted information and the chance to process it on their own, through their own unique generational lens. When leaders engage the middle, that group's priorities shift, bringing quiet discontent to the forefront and increasing an organization's resilience and positivity.

In today's raging world, where gaining our attention seems to be everyone's goal, we've become much more comfortable with what we want to hear, what pleases us, what is easiest, or anything else that sparks the validation we think we deserve—so much so that the truth has become a stranger that we suspect isn't real. But by demanding 100% of the truth, we can pull together to find our way around obstacles, because we better understand what they are. We can see that emergence is a viable option and that we can provide sustenance for and allocate resources to growing ideas. Through this strategy we gain greater understanding, create strategies for expansion and acceptance, interact with people as whole beings, and support initiatives that invite others in. Not only will truth reveal what has robbed us of possibility; it will also help us begin to shed what no longer works while exposing blockages and misalignments. This is where the truth unifies—not on the edges, but in the center.

While the initial revelation of truth can make us uncomfortable, ashamed, or even scared, it enables us to regroup around what is real—to collectively commit to being all in and truly rely on and respect one another. The shift that operating in truth brings is palpable. With

100% of the truth in play, we can better understand how vital we are to the whole of what is happening, and all involved begin to recognize that their organization is calling on their best. A vision of a different and better future state begins to emerge, even when you're already pretty content with where you are. Likewise, those on the extremes can better see where they align, and may ask how they can join in the shared efforts. It also makes clear what, and sometimes who, needs to go.

Probably the greatest shift in the presence of truth that moves us toward better outcomes and elevated performance is an almost natural letting go of fear. We stop wasting energy on what "may" be happening or what our role "might be" in the action. Even when the worst news is the truth, we can begin to prepare, better determining our options and chiseling out new pathways. There is nothing worse than a board that is unwilling or incapable of sharing the full truth with leaders. All that happens is that leaders build the future based on what they know to be true, instead of what *is* true. When the truth finally becomes illuminated, the trust is forever destroyed, and so, too, is performance.

THE ART OF DECEPTION

Often, leaders work around the truth, applying assumptions, track records, and market knowledge. They use only the typical 80% of truth because they possess an outdated understanding that we're supposed to know it all, that we alone must figure it out, and if we don't watch out for ourselves, who else will? The more we believe we're "right," the more we build walls that begin to imprison us in the half-truths of our own making. The process starts when we first deceive ourselves, then dig in and defend the truth that makes us the least fearful. Sun Tzu, the great Chinese military strategist, believed that "all war is based on deception." By that logic, when we deceive ourselves through not clearly understanding our role in an event or lacking understanding about our capabilities, we may not realize that puts us at war with ourselves. We carry that inner war into battle with others as we project our wants, needs, and convictions, convincing ourselves that our position or version of the truth is the right one, rather than seeing truth as input that feeds a whole understanding.

Self-deception—be it in the form of ego and overconfidence around our abilities, personal biases that close us off to others, or the imposter syndrome and the fear associated with leading in an ever-evolving world—often causes leaders to be lost. As noted, self-deceptors are the internal forces that impede us and hinder our leadership potential. They can harm our interactions with others, reducing our abilities to foster cultures of belonging where everyone can thrive.

CONNECT FEAR AND TRUST

In many corporate cultures, fear is layered, both as felt throughout the organization as well as your own. This can leave you siloed to focus on the problems, cut off from support and counsel.

Research suggests that fear in organizations boosts risk by eating away at people's self-esteem and team cohesiveness, yielding increased stress and helplessness. Fear also makes us less likely to report our mistakes and more likely to continue making the same errors. The Society for Human Resource Management's Politics at Work survey demonstrated that nearly half of American employees surveyed had personally experienced political disagreements in the workplace, and one-third said that their workplace is not accepting of differing political perspectives. Many organizations want to create psychological safety by balancing fear and trust, but they do not understand how to do so without having psychological safety come at the expense of the truth. The result is silence. And silence can be deadly. Look no further than companies where workplace accidents have actually killed people because the truth was not prioritized, encouraged, or supported. This shows how suppressing the truth literally kills employees in the safety sense, but it is harder to see how this silence can kill ideas, relationships, and results. But kill them it does.

Part of seeking 100% of the truth is a willingness to ask the right questions and challenge the existing, traditional functions and power structures. Why? Because they exist. And, given the continuing change around us, we have a responsibility to challenge everything. When we are unwilling to push outside our comfort zone, we allow the truth to hover in areas that should make us feel uncomfortable. Often those are the very areas where truth is most needed.

Take the traditional human resource function. Why shouldn't we ask whether the current HR construct is right? Most often it is not, but people are unwilling to seek the full truth. Yet, ask regular employees (as we do, across thousands of companies) who in the office they don't trust, and often they will say HR, because it is set up not to support the people it is supposed to serve, but to punish them and push policy onto them. HR must return to being about people—individual people with individual needs. And while HR is in the process of transformation, the commitment to people must come from the top of an organization: the CEO and the board. Are we putting our most vocal advocates for people in a place to succeed? The answer is an overwhelming no. These advocates are too often saddled with upholding policy over people. This is backwards. Doing right for and by people must trump all else. We also cannot place the DEI function under HR and expect the organization to embrace it. We have already identified HR as a place for compliance, not for growth, understanding, and creating a diverse yet unified whole. Therefore we cannot unite the functions under one department.

In HR as well as throughout the organization, leaders must get to the truths of what our people need to thrive. We must face the Great Disconnect and change our current understanding and past norms. It is not fair for the newest in the workforce to be the lone challengers—the experienced and most tenured in the organization should share that responsibility. As a leader, you need to ask yourself if you are open to the truth as it influences and affects your organization. What other areas besides HR are limiting the truth? Communications? Legal? Barriers to the truth exist in all companies—and often it is leaders who have created and perpetuate them.

When it comes to belonging, we cannot settle for the majority opinion or the first idea. If we do, we get stuck in our biased ways of thinking, revert toward sameness in thought and actions, and avoid difficult but necessary challenging conversations. To create cultures of belonging, we should instead invite dissenting voices into the dialogue and ensure we devote sufficient time, energy, and resources to uncovering the missing, omitted percentage of truth. We mistakenly believe that these voices are only in the extremes—they are not. More likely, they are found in the moveable middle. The middle may be quieter, but instead of voicing views loudly, they quietly hold on to them until they walk away.

Everyone should feel safe speaking up, even if they lack certainty about the topic at hand and have lingering questions. It is too easy to walk away from the full truth or omit facts. When we look at the Holocaust Museum Houston story, it reminds us of how easy it is to turn away and not contribute, for somebody else to fill in the gaps while we just stay out of it. Such avoidance creates an even larger gap in understanding and ultimately delays acceptance. Without stepping in and up, we are fostering misunderstanding and mistruth, thus limiting the ability to genuinely belong. Belonging takes courage; it requires us to be in the discomfort, recognizing that sometimes when we step up, it means that we can no longer belong to a space that we once occupied but where we no longer fit.

When organizations accumulate layers of partial truths, they perpetuate all kinds of misrepresentations, falsehoods, and outright lies. We used to call this "office politics," but where we are now feels darker than that emotionally loaded term, as we strive for more balance and joy in our work and lives. Today's world alone can unnerve us and throw us into some sort of collective survival instinct. We are left wondering if our leaders have lost their gumption to lead and if they, too, feel fear.

Belonging calls for us to strip away these layers of half-truths and reveal the remaining 20% of truth, which may seem unrecognizable for not having been told for so long.

Without belonging, it's difficult to have vulnerability, the foundation upon which trust and psychological safety are built. Belonging enables us to feel safe enough to be vulnerable, to be our authentic selves in a world where dismissing or hiding from the truth is the norm. When we feel like we belong, we're able to share our perspectives without fear or dismissal, making us more likely to continue being truthful. Belonging creates a feedback loop for truth to come out. Human-focused problems are complex and can increase the time that belonging requires to emerge. Without the comfort that safety brings, we are less inclined to collaborate, solve problems, or share perspectives. Without trust, mutated truth leaks out as criticism and complaining, with undertones of dissatisfaction.

Living and working in partnership fed by truth fans our faith in self and trust in others. In that intentional space, we begin to do the real work toward having what we need, when we need it, certain that we can unite to get us where our vision, dreams, and goals take us. Together, we can build a bridge to help, advocate, and protect one another; to lay claim to what is ours to claim; and to be seen and heard—to be fully realized in all versions of our capacity. We can keep growing and expanding. In an ecosphere of belonging, truth is the oxygen, an essential element upon which recalibration, possibility, and opportunity for all relies.

I often think about how we at Deutser ensure that our clients and I are working in 100% of the truth. We teach leaders to pose three basic questions to themselves and others in the room in the most challenging conversations:

- Have I been honest with myself? (Inward facing)
- Have I asked the questions and listened to different perspectives to encourage the full truth? (Outward facing)

- What is one thing I/we can do or say to add to a fuller conversation? (For all)

IMPLEMENTING 100% OF THE TRUTH

Akbar Mohammed, president of one of the two largest AT&T franchise retailers in the country, saw that by leveraging 100% of the truth, his organization, Prime Communications, could successfully bridge the acquisition of a larger, high-culture Mormon-led company with their smaller Muslim-owned company. The merger created a single entity with more than 2,000 stores in more than 40 states across the country. The challenge was to create one cohesive whole from two companies with vastly different cultures. The smaller, acquiring company was Muslim owned, valuing operations over people and valuing scrappiness as a defining characteristic. By contrast, the larger, acquired company was Mormon led and operated (with headquarters in Salt Lake City), and had invested deeply in a robust, inclusive, people-centric culture.

When my firm came in to consult, the only way to describe the relationship between the two leadership teams was as excessively vitriolic. Dislike and mistrust defined their interactions. Akbar recalls the situation: "We saw that leadership needed to be able to make decisions faster with individuals who weren't open to us. Pockets of leaders who weren't with us from the beginning needed to trust us immediately." What Akbar felt, we saw and experienced firsthand. So, after our team conducted extensive diagnostics on both companies, including more than 150 individual interviews, we brought the two leadership teams together for an open, honest, and revealing discussion.

We were aware that this was a battle of culture versus operations, which unfortunately was manifesting as Mormon versus Muslim throughout the companies and within their leadership teams. Lost in the crossfire were the people in the middle who followed neither faith and just wanted a reasonably decent place to work and belong.

Ironically, employees from each company felt like their respective companies had provided this before the merger. But after the companies joined, battle lines were drawn.

Forcing the leaders to hear the real, unvarnished opinions of these "others" in a nonthreatening environment changed everything. We asked each member of the new leadership team to write down five questions about the new company. Our only stipulation was that each question needed to start with "Why . . ." Our team then read aloud each of the more than one hundred anonymous questions we received. The science behind this format is that the questions now belong to the facilitator instead of individuals within an organization. Our purpose was to turn directly toward extremes that seemed entrenched and reveal 100% of the truth through open exchange.

We began reading the questions one by one. A sample: "Why do Muslims not value culture?" "Why are Mormons intolerant of anyone different from them?" "Why do they not consider that their 'We're all about people' BS is covering for their lack of business intellect?" Based on the questions and postures of the people in the room, it was clear that neither group wanted any form of resolution. They had come to have their say and stand their ground with no appetite for conciliation. Each wanted to outwait the other.

It was Akbar, the youngest of the leaders and the second-largest shareholder of the combined company, who broke through, by having the courage to answer the most aggressive and hateful of the questions. He stood tall, made eye contact with as many in the room as possible, and both admitted to and led an exchange on the deficiencies in his own company. His sharing 100% of his truth made space for others to be open about their religion, their business philosophy, and the areas that were harming their business success. He answered every question, looking each person in the eye.

Akbar recalls, "Before this exchange, everyone was talking in code, within their familiar culture. Their image of us was as 'cheap.' What we considered as 'hunger for success' they saw as 'overly aggressive.'"

Pulling back the curtain between the two company cultures in this fashion opened a way to a shared, cohesive, enterprise identity where they could come together over shared goals, values, and dreams of success. They committed to their intentions with agreed-on, measurable outcomes that became a critical anchor for all. To this end, the company created unique dashboards for individual and team performance so everyone knew exactly where they stood at any given time. The effort was grounded in truth—in data. This operational approach began to attract performance-driven individuals from all levels of the company.

Agility in leadership became crucial as all worked together to mentor and coach underperformers. They learned to include multiple opinions on how to enhance performance and solve local store concerns, because each store presented its own ecosphere that expressed the characteristics of its local community. The entire organization has made it a priority to see that the diversity and participation of their staff reflects the communities within which they work. Leadership also developed an open communication policy. "Be approachable" was their mission. Any employee could come to anyone on the leadership team directly, including Akbar. "I get 30–40 text messages daily from employees where they can share any concerns, any ideas. Any manager can pull up the individual's dashboard and we can talk about results in real time and what might be impacting those results, both positively and negatively. Employees see me as accessible, very available, and believe I work hard to make sure they have a place to be in five, ten, fifteen, twenty years in communities where they live."

Akbar's leadership philosophy is "'You serve them,' not 'they serve you.'" He is demanding but clear in his expectations. He promotes from within. Akbar expects adherence and adoption to the "Prime Way," the company's cultural bible. He provides a defined career ladder and tools so employees know every step ahead. Everyone knows that everything is measured. It is a high-stakes sales environment, but within an ecosphere of support and exchange.

In the first year after Deutser's engagement, Prime experienced increased employee happiness, productivity, and retention of more than 50% across all locations, even as other businesses followed the national retail trend of mass resignations. This retention improvement increased operational success and added millions of dollars to the bottom line. Most importantly, it reinforced what happens when a courageous and determined leader puts 100% of the truth at the forefront.

GETTING TO THE TRUTH

Beyond intentionality, patience, and continued practice, I find the following considerations to be particularly helpful for getting to 100% of the truth:

1. **Be in a safe environment, even when you are not.** This means putting yourself in a place to have conversations conducive to a whole approach to the truth. Even if you don't share initially, don't avoid the conversation. Exposing yourself to ideas and discourse that make you uncomfortable will build your tolerance and ability to find a way into the conversation. Keep showing up. Think about what you would say if you felt more comfortable. Then, if you feel unsafe, trust yourself and share the truth at another time and place.

2. **Start with a question, then lean into clarifying questions** to keep the dialogue going and encourage sharing of alternative perspectives. "Can you help me understand?" "What are we trying to answer or address?" "How can we accept a different outcome?" There are many ways to be open and to invite others to share in that openness.

3. **Find common ground.** Can you identify anything you both share? This can be about the situation you are discussing or a broader topic, such as human characteristics. For example,

you both want to share your views of the same situation, so you agree to do so.

4. **Lead with facts and not emotion.** When we turn the heat up with feelings, it is difficult to return to a more objective approach. Start with facts, check in to see if these facts can be agreed on, and work to build a base from this agreement. If you can't get to this basic level of agreement, work on discovering where the gap is and bring in more information that addresses it.

5. **State the obvious first.** Withholding things that might seem clear to all can nonetheless influence your discussion or perspective. To avoid this, create a hierarchy for spelling out the truth, starting with the most obvious elephants in the room.

6. **Don't fight in the moment.** Truth, as with so many elements of belonging, can be layered. Getting to the truth takes time. Don't seek a quick knockout win; this process is about the thoughtful sharing of difficult information. Fighting only pushes people to their corners, where they hold tight to their long-held beliefs. Instead, give people space to accept your thoughts by not pushing them away. The space for belonging has room for many ideas and perspectives.

7. **Accept that the truth, based in fact, may differ from what you first believed or were told.** Few things are absolute and there is not always a right and a wrong.

8. **Get to the productive truth, not the destructive variety.** We can push too hard and get so personal that even the truth becomes unpalatable. Stick with respect, positive contributions, and understanding instead of deploying zingers, breaking confidences, and increasing the hurt.

9. **Share truth with the intent for discourse.** Whatever truth you choose to share, be open to the conversation that follows. In fact, be intentional about setting up a space for it. This

brings people in and allows for belonging in the discussion. Also, don't drop a bombshell right before the conversation is wrapping up or all parties reach some agreement.

RECONCILING WITH THE TRUTH

We owe it to those around us to provide the full truth but with respect. The truth may hurt, but we don't ever have to cause further hurt by how we deliver it. We do a greater disservice by withholding it. Think about the times we choose not to tell a colleague or employee about their poor performance. We are withholding the very information they need to make their own decision. Truth serves as a connector, even when it is difficult to deliver or accept. Putting the truth out front enables the necessary discourse and debate that actually brings people together. Without it, we are left wondering, "What else do I need to know?"

There is a great deal of courage in seeking and sharing our truths, a courage that we can't avoid and instead must actively fight for in ourselves and in others to achieve genuine connection. Belonging reflects an ability to hold space for the truth. This process can be messy and stressful, but it's the only way we learn how to build bridges with people who are different from us instead of continuing to remain isolated in our echo chambers.

As we reconcile with the truth, we also must begin the necessary reconnection and recalibration with the middle. The middle is where our power lies and our future takes hold. It is here that we begin the necessary reconnection while rebuilding for the future. It is where we nurture and buoy belonging. By listening to but not overreacting to the extremes, and more fully engaging the moveable middle, we will create an organic movement that builds unity, encourages safe spaces to operate, and supports the most critical and often stable part of your organization. The middle will demand the truth quietly, process the truth internally, and act on the truth through their work and actions. They may not be as vocal or out front as the extremes, but they will do what needs to be done—and when you back it with 100% of the truth, they will do it not their way, but the shared organizational way—your way. This empowers the leader to begin to not only serve but also strengthen their silent weapon—the middle. Arriving at 100% of the truth takes courageous leadership, but it's vital for the trust that drives belonging.

FINDING PERSPECTIVE

Throughout your life, you will need to be able to see different perspectives—usually at the same time. Answer the questions below to challenge your way of thinking.

_____

How many different things do you see in this image?

_____

Do you see the cubes or boxes?

_____

Do you see the black as the top or bottom of the box? Can you see both?

_____

What do the clouds represent for you?_____

_____

Can you think of a time when you saw something and someone might have seen it differently than you?

_____

What can you do the next time a colleague or friend sees something different than you?

_____

DEMAND 100% OF THE TRUTH

Identify a time when you led with 100% of the truth.

_____
_____

What compelled you to lead with 100% of the truth? How hard was it for you?

_____
_____

How did people respond?

_____
_____

What was the outcome? Looking back, would you do anything differently?

_____
_____
_____
_____
_____

Now, think of a time when you didn't lead with 100% of the truth. Why did you or others choose to leave information out? How did it change the outcome?

_____
_____
_____
_____
_____

How did you feel knowing there was more to include, but it was withheld?

_____
_____
_____
_____
_____

How might the situation have changed if you had considered the three leadership questions and the considerations on getting to 100% of the truth posed in this chapter?

_____
_____
_____
_____
_____

Chapter 6

LEADER OF YOU

LEVERAGING THE RULES FOR LEADERS

There is a collective outcry for human-centered leaders who cement cultures of belonging in their organizations. Leaders are being forced to navigate the swirl of constant change in their personal and professional lives with consequences and outcomes at every turn. Unlike previous times in history, the intensity of the evolving societal and political forces affecting our personal, professional, and family lives have us constantly alert, driven by fear, retreating, and at times afraid to act. Nobody can, or should, lead when their operational pre-set is "Maybe this will just go away" or "I hope this doesn't happen to me."

The belonging leader takes a different perspective: "I want to embrace this, call this out, and start solving this, or learn more about it before it manifests into something different." Simply hoping something doesn't happen sets you up to live an accidental outcome. Most of us do this daily without even thinking about it. When we find ourselves afraid to go deep, resisting the need to turn *in* to difficulty and face it directly, we're hiding from our innate ability to thrive and grow while advancing others along with us.

To be effective today and tomorrow, and twenty years from now, a leader must first deeply understand how to lead themselves. Without that understanding of your own leadership, you will continue doing things that look like leadership but may not empower you to reach your fullest potential. And, when that happens, leaders all too often leave people behind or, worse, out. Reflect for a moment on whom you are leading first: the team or yourself. The leader of you—the only label I believe is appropriate for each of us, regardless of your role, title, or place in life—requires more than your people; it requires you to prioritize yourself first.

UNDERSTANDING YOURSELF FIRST

At Deutser, we reject deficit-based leadership and see the value in building upon what is already working, helping leaders understand growth through their strengths. Aligning with our perspective on leading the self, I'm going to take you through a series of insightful and sometimes probing questions and exercises in this chapter that will help you to better explore your own leadership style and begin to populate your personal leadership profile. Building your understanding of the leader of you encourages you to go deeper than the typical "who am I?" Through this self-exploration, we can achieve profound growth.

Question who you *really* are and what you value as a leader. What differentiates your leadership? How do you reconcile DEI and identity? How do you tether your efforts to a more relevant, sustainable leadership? How do you make sense of competing perspectives (e.g., generational, gendered, racial, cultural, political)? How do you actively leverage positivity not as a mindset but a leadership competency? How do you balance the need for truth and transparency amid the threat of erasure? How do you challenge everything, including a potentially antiquated attachment to winning and losing? How do you approach belonging and bringing people into your space? How do you turn in to power and challenge?

Your answer to these questions will differ at different times in your life. Our consultants are trained to see patterns in leaders. To the degree a leader is committed to understanding these areas, the greater likelihood they will have of sustaining success and producing longer-term and more systemic change in their organizations and communities. And the more they will embrace the concepts around what it means to be a belonging leader.

The leader of us and within us relishes challenge. We actively hunt for it and are energized to tackle it head on. We do not back away from challenge; rather, we embrace it. But, sometimes, we get so stuck in the rut of everyday leadership that we put aside for a day, a week, or more the differentiating concepts that define who we are and what we want from our own leadership. To equip you for these moments, this chapter offers exercises, stories, and explorations to make sure you are aligned as the leader you want and need to be—not for others, but for you. We will challenge you to think about what leadership means to you and how belonging leadership aligns with your current leadership style, goals, and expectations of others and yourself.

Great leaders perpetually search for something more. This search, and their passion for what is next, takes them to interesting places—often, back to the most important place, themselves. We have found the most powerful excursion a leader can take is rarely organizational and almost always personal.

It is the great leaders who discover that the best and truest form of leadership lies deep inside each of them—ready to be rediscovered, reoriented, repurposed, and redesigned for today's challenges. The answers lie within the leader of you.

THE LEADERSHIP TETHER

Leadership doesn't start at a certain time. It is a current that runs throughout our lives, our experiences, and our decisions. It is always evolving. For most of us, it is a continual growth trajectory that is tethered to our past experiences. How we understand those experiences propels us forward to the leader we are going to become. We reject the premise that leaders are born, not made. Instead, we acknowledge that leaders are born *and* made. I believe everyone is born to lead one—yourself, thus the leader of you. The capacity to lead more people is then determined by your continual reflection, work, and growth.

The foundations and fundamentals for leadership are often evident at a young age. Yet, when we work with leaders, they talk about their more recent leadership experiences first, because they seem more substantial or relevant. Many of us ignore our early experiences and how they inform later decisions through our style of leadership, especially regarding how and what we trust in ourselves and others. After all, most of us are bombarded by the "What have you done for me lately?" mentality in leadership that never slows down enough to let us off the merry-go-round of proving ourselves. Reflecting on the influence of experiences and exposure to input and ideas that have brought you to where you are today is an interesting exercise.

The leadership tether is an accessible, important tool that leaders can use to intentionally consider the entirety of their leadership—past, present, and future. Sound like a familiar plot to a classic holiday story? Sometimes you need an awakening to see your patterns and reignite earlier fires within you that stoked earlier successes. The leadership tether will provide a thoughtful inventory of your earliest experiences, your wins and losses, your high and low points, and all that influenced your way here, where you are now.

The tether is personal. I am asked, "What made you put what you did on your tether?" My tether is made up of awards, recognitions, leadership highlights and lowlights, accomplishments, milestones, and life events that have shaped and defined me as a leader. There are so many important things in my life that have supported (and at times derailed) me as a leader, even if they were just moments. I have learned that by identifying them and putting them on paper, I can connect past experiences to the way I lead today and to the leader I plan to become. The tether has been central to how I think about belonging. It creates a picture of where I fit, where I did not fit, and where I invited people in and left them out. The experiences provide an undeniable measure of clarity of who I have been as a genuine belonging leader.

It is why I started my leadership tether with my earliest memory of leadership: being given the "Best Rester Award" in kindergarten and earning my first paycheck at seven years old (Royal Homes, $7). It was the first time that I remember being recognized, regardless of what the recognition was for. There are other points of recognition on my tether, including receiving humanitarian awards, being recognized on National Philanthropy Day, or being selected to lead challenging work. Recording them on a tether reveals the interconnectedness that links each of these experiences to the nuanced and challenging work I do today.

The following sections categorize some of the other defining moments of my tether.

Experiencing Personal Belonging

There are experiences on my tether that launched great periods of belonging for me and, by extension, others. I think about my eleven years working at Camp Greylock, one of the oldest private boys' camps in the country, where I worked in various leadership capacities to coach, teach, and mentor hundreds of young men. Those experiences were the precursors for my work coaching athletes, leading the Houston Texans' cultural transformation, guiding a controversial intergenerational strategic conversation at Holocaust Museum Houston, and finally gaining membership in the Young Presidents' Organization. There are other experiences that highlight belonging:

- It may seem counterintuitive that someone who coaches elite executives across the world would be intimidated by coaching elite college athletes—but that is what happened when I first began coaching players—that is, until they immediately brought me in and made me feel part of the team.
- One of the earliest and most transformational experiences in my professional career came shortly after I was fired from my job with a wife, two children under three years old, and a new dream house. I was aggressively recruited to work for a Historically Black University. Surprisingly, it became my first client.

Experiencing Being an Outsider

I have grown so much in life through the too-many times that I was left out, ignored, or not invited inside. It started with being rejected by sixty-one companies when I was a senior in college. No one would hire me. Then, after I "retired" early from law school (a fancy way to say I quit after my second year), my parents forced me to pass my résumé out on the streets of Houston day after day for six weeks. It was humiliating and life changing all in one.

The Value of Taking Inventory: Defining Leadership Moments

I also like to think about the defining moments in my life through the perspective of acceleration and deceleration points. These are the times that either slowed me down or propelled me in very different ways forward, and all changed the trajectory of my career. Examples include having been fired not once but twice, shoveling elephant poop for the circus, buying out my business partner and going out on my own, and rejecting the opportunity to buy my dream summer camp after it was offered to me because I thought I was too young.

Those are moments that catapulted my career in different directions. Other transformational moments include being selected to lead

LEADERSHIP TETHER

CREATE YOUR LEADERSHIP TETHER

Write on the lines as many experiences from your life as you can that have contributed to being the leader you are today. Think about very early experiences, memories, awards, wins, losses, starts, stops, defining moments, transitions, etc. This is **YOUR** leadership tether—so make it as robust and full as possible. Challenge yourself to find experiences in every life phase.

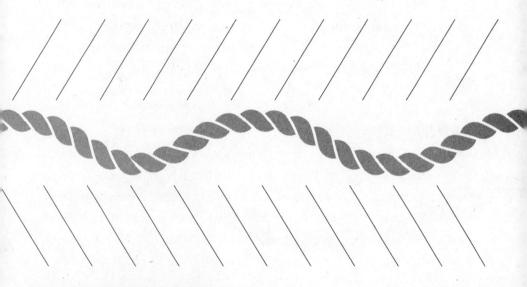

BELONGING

A sense of belonging is integral in teamwork, leadership, and success. Here is how we define what belonging looks like.

- LISTEN WITHOUT LABELS

- IDENTITY OVER PURPOSE

- TURN IN TO THE POWER

- CHALLENGE EVERYTHING

- 100% OF THE TRUTH

EXERCISE

Identify your top five transformative leadership moments on your leadership tether by circling them. Once you've identified your top five moments, ask yourself these questions.

Where did I feel I belonged the most?

_____

Where did I feel I belonged the least?

_____

Did any experience create space for others to belong?

_____

As a leader, how do I create a sense of belonging moving forward?

_____

LEADERSHIP TETHER

Early Years 4–19
- Best Rester Award
- First paycheck, Royal Homes, $7
- Made "A" basketball team
- Bar mitzvah
- Simon Margolis Humanitarian Award
- *Bye Bye Birdie* star
- Lieutenant in Color War
- Counselor
- Varsity basketball
- Varsity baseball
- Accepted to college
- First night at college
- Joined fraternity (forced by parents)
- Group leader for 70+ 15-year-old boys

Early Twenties
- Head judge, Red and Gray Color War
- Director of basketball at cam
- Senior side group leader
- Won Pittsfield Boys Club Tournament
- Won Greylock 16.0 Invitational
- Graduated from college
- Hired for first job
- Top leasing agent
- Fired from Judwin Properties
- Study abroad in London
- Solicitor in London (largest robbery in history of Great Britain)
- Accepted to law school
- Coached high school basketball

Early Forties
- Hired first employee (ever!)
- Partnership with Yaffe (Yaffe|Deutser)
- Recognized by National Philanthropy Day
- Became president of large family foundation
- Coached kids' basketball, football, and soccer
- Managed kerfuffle at school
- Rejected for consideration of membership at club: "not ready for people like you"
- Bubble-wrapped-ambulance experiment
- Reorganized Yaffe|Deutser
- Bought out my partners
- Opened Deutser (strategy, culture, and communication)
- Hosted major event with Shawn Achor
- Lost home to mold

Late Forties
- Managed multiple fatal aviation accident aftermaths
- Created safety survey with Shawn Achor
- Designed and hosted YPO Couples' Retreat
- Created Warren Buffett event
- Design and architect of Wolff Center for Entrepreneurship
- YPO Learning Chair
- School Board of Trustees
- Shawn Achor telling me to write a book
- Writing and thought partner agreeing to write with me
- Barbara Bush strategy
- Conduct Ms. Lorraine's funeral
- Wrote *Leading Clarity*
- *Today Show* appearance
- Became best-selling author (*LA Times*)

Late Twenties

- Retired early from law school (2 years)
- Turned down opportunity to buy Greylock
- Passed résumés in downtown Houston
- Ringling Bros. job (grew territory + corporate fight)
- Shoveling elephant poop—Great Pachyderm Poo Giveaway (first media opp)
- Walt Disney World on Ice success! (Peter Pan)
- Traded for Christmas lobster dinner with girlfriend
- Resigned from Ringling (turning down corporate job)
- Hired as only man at all-female firm
- Article in *Boston Globe* (quoted me)
- Fired from Reebok (client)
- Created the Pittard's Stay Soft Challenge
- Hired at marketing and advertising agency in Houston

Thirties

- Got married
- Deutser's Defeating Diabetes Walk team chair
- Joined entrepreneur organization
- President, Leaders of Tomorrow, UT Health Science Center
- Promoted to Senior Creative Group Director
- Had first child
- Invited to be member of Children's Fund
- Gala chair, Children's Fund
- Charity selection for Children's Fund
- President, Children's Fund
- Had second child
- Fired from marketing and advertising agency
- TSU demand—work for them or be first client
- Started J. Bradley Partners

Fifty+

- Birthed Deutser Clarity Institute
- Became speaker and expert facilitator
- Holocaust Museum culture and future, facilitator ("hard to hate up close")
- Selected to be president of Wolff Foundation
- Debuted the *Way* book concept
- Redesigned Deutser (human approach to change)
- Invested in major new experiential space
- Selected to be YPO president
- Accepted into selective club
- Published whitepaper (positivity)
- Designed hedge fund and Learning Lab
- Survived COVID and grew business (publishing strategy)
- "Eyes" interviews and community discussions
- "Eyes" committee and report/videos
- Unfavorable article
- University culture work
- Healthcare Marketing Communications chair
- Negotiation and agreement on issue
- Institute open in NYC
- Partnership and institute open in Bermuda

More Fifty+

- 100,000+ singing "Eyes of Texas" at first home game
- Designed University of Arizona (UA) football culture
- Redesigned Houston Texans Football organization
- Redesigned University of Arizona football experience and facility
- Opened University of Arizona Sports Performance Institute (Fifth Quarter)
- Coached first class of athletes at UA
- First win as leadership coach for UA team
- Confront publisher
- Recruiting role for football program
- Lost longest tenured contract after 17 years
- Wrote second book
- Rejected by publisher
- Selected publisher
- Redesigned anti-hazing, healthy organization curriculum
- Leading effort to define university culturer
- Redesigned Deutser and company ecosystem
- UA 4th win
- Birthed Belonging Lab Concept (Institute for Belonging)

an inquiry into "The Eyes of Texas" and invited in to head the cultural renaissance of a Division I football program and an NFL team.

Most leaders have a lifetime of experiences that have positioned them to be where they are. It is important to pause to take inventory of the whole of your past as you work in real time to accelerate your leadership forward.

WINNING AND LOSING

My tether is littered with wins and losses—even if they are not categorized that way. In fact, winning and losing is one of my favorite leadership topics—and often the one that is least dissected and discussed. I find it fascinating to work with leaders at all levels and enjoy delving into their psyches to determine what fuels them more: the thrill of the win or the agony of the loss.

Personally, I want and expect the win every single time. It is the loss that eats away at me. I never fear losing because I never expect to lose. Someone may have more talent, they may perform better on a given day, but I don't think about it as a loss unless I didn't give every bit of effort I had. But losses are part of leadership and life. Some leaders don't think about the win or the loss and are solely driven by the competition. They find their joy from being in the battle—and that is where they stay. When the the stakes are the highest, they just want to be in the arena. By contrast, I have a competitive nature that wants to win every time, and I thrive on the competition—even when it is a simple as someone telling me "No" or "You can't do that." Watch me.

How I feel about wins and losses arises intuitively from my playing and coaching sports, owning and operating businesses, and living through challenging ups and downs in life. But it wasn't until I elevated this attitude to front of mind, during a period when I felt under siege, that I reconsidered it from a work standpoint. I was working on a project with national implications. The media was on the attack and informing anyone who read their articles or posts that we were losing the battle and the hearts and minds of the people. I had not thought about it that way; I was deep in the "competition," doing my work, attempting to blunt every attack. It was an intense fight, day after day. I never thought about winning or losing, just doing.

That is, until I got a call from a friend who challenged me with simple words: "How does it feel to be getting your ass kicked? How do you feel about everyone knowing you are losing and losing big?"

I was devastated. I never thought about it like that. After all, I was in the battle, and we weren't even 75% of the way through the project. I felt derailed and demoralized in the moment.

After deep reflection, I got angry. I realized that others' perceptions of my losing was wrong—they were basing it on the extremist's perspective. Through that lens, they were right. But my goal was to move the middle and lead that group with information. When I recalibrated my perspective, I realized that I was actually winning the game I wanted, needed, and was hired to win. It shows how sometimes we allow ourselves to lose focus and let others define our personal scoreboard.

Right or wrong, professional and collegiate sports have become about winning only. It can be destructive without the necessary checks and balances, including how they win and lose.

We challenge coaches and leaders to define their framework around this concept and think about the personal scoreboard that they not only carry around every day in their minds, but are responsible for operating 24-7. Leaders constantly keep score and manipulate the scoreboard to tell their story—whatever it may be in a given moment. Am I advancing in my company fast enough, is the bottom line big enough, do I have enough power, is my voice strong enough, am I making enough money? We cannot let others define our scoreboards—otherwise we would lose every day. The scoreboard I have chosen is about what I give and how much I support—not what I make in terms of money; yours in turn should reflect the things that motivate you. In the NFL, I work with leaders to focus on the everyday wins—those we have the most control over. Every day, every person in the organization has a chance to win or achieve or accomplish something great. I am happy to stack those daily wins and measure them. As I tell the organization, if you can win on 348 days, it makes it a lot easier to have success on the 17 days that you compete on the field.

Leaders must choose an approach that is healthy and real. Too often the game that is lost is the game never played—the game in our minds. Approximately eighty thousand thoughts go through the mind of a leader each day. Most are not real, yet often we process them through a negative lens, which convinces us we are losing. This thought pattern takes us out of the current moment and keeps us in an unbalanced cycle where we're always playing catch-up or thinking we are behind. At times this is helpful, but often it robs us of one of our superpowers: positivity.

POSITIVITY, PERFORMANCE, AND THE LEADER OF YOU

Positivity is the foundation of leadership. It serves as one of the most vital connectors of people, companies, and relationships. It is the glue that binds companies and individuals to a desired future state and holds strong organizations together. Yet, for many leaders, positivity is grossly misunderstood, misapplied and, mistakenly, not measured.

Positivity is a precious resource, something leaders can lean on to help them function better not only in the workplace, but outside of it as well. Positivity allows us to expand our thought processes, ideas, beliefs, and actions. The optimism and mindfulness that characterize a positive state of being encourage us to problem-solve and become more inclusive. Further, the ability to handle adverse events and remain self-confident in the wake of negative experiences, due to maintaining a positive and emotionally agile attitude, isn't to be taken lightly. Positivity is something we all need to tap into, particularly in ambiguous and uncertain times.

Positivity can boost employee engagement by improving efficiency and profits while reducing turnover, burnout, and absenteeism. It is a critical resource that allows the CEO and leadership team to accurately assess employee engagement and, ultimately, collective performance. As I have worked with leaders across a myriad of industries to effect organizational change and transformation, I've seen how positivity becomes not simply a "rah-rah" moment but rather a deeply scientific tactic to redirect and psychologically influence the organization. But first, it must be understood.

Here, we describe several of the researchers' key findings on the positivity–performance link, followed by strategies for organizations and leaders to pursue. My team of researchers has studied positivity in the workforce for decades to understand the elements that comprise it as well as to create the metrics and tools to measure it within organizations. We approach positivity as five distinct dimensions that, once activated, further engage and shift the organizational attitudes and beliefs around positivity and, ultimately, belonging.

The five dimensions of positivity are:

Inspiration: The ability to motivate and lift up

Mindfulness: The ability to be fully present and aware in the moment

Happiness: The ability to feel a sense of joy

Optimism: The ability to anticipate the best possible outcome

Gratitude: The quality of being thankful

Leaders can evaluate these dimensions on a personal and organizational scope. The five aspects make positivity measurable, understandable (quantitatively and qualitatively), and actionable using specific strategic levers. One of these, the Positivity Quotient, developed by social scientists at Deutser, is a highly predictive research assessment that accurately measures positivity across all five dimensions. Here, we describe several of our research team's key findings on the positivity–performance link, followed by strategies for organizations and leaders to pursue (you can find this research at www.deutser.com).

- This study of about 3,800 employees across industries and sectors showed that positivity is a core driver of organizational performance and predicts a company's ability to achieve its desired future state more efficiently.
- Positivity is a crucial ingredient in fostering organizational culture. Our research team demonstrated that focusing efforts on positivity encourages more favorable perceptions of teamwork, talent management, coaching and development, fit, and organizational climate. Taken together, our conceptualization of organizational culture arises from these dimensions, and positivity is a paramount predictor of success across them.
- Teamwork is the greatest and strongest predictor of positivity. It is key for leaders who foster strong learning orientations, collective team cultures, and psychologically safe environments where team members experience mutual respect, trust, and a sense of belonging.
- The power of positivity extends beyond boosting employee morale. Positivity is also instrumental in supporting the strategic system, informing the overall direction and operations of the company, as well as its ability to adapt to change and achieve its business objectives.
- Positivity has a tangible, measurable effect on business outcomes. There is a conclusive connection between

positivity, Employer Net Performance Scores, employee engagement, and organizational performance.

- There is also a direct correlation between positivity and belonging. The higher the Positivity Quotient, the higher the perceived sense of belonging.

POSITIVITY IN PRACTICE

Why is this important? Leading with optimism and engaging in positive interventions leads to better outcomes, including reduced burnout, greater optimism about work, increased connectedness within the organization, and favorable perceptions that the organization is heading in the right direction. Deutser research also validates that positivity is a predictor of future success. Our work clearly demonstrates the link between positivity and performance.

All of this contributes to an elevated sense of inclusion and belonging. Our team of researchers conducted an experiment with a diverse sample of employees, finding that people will choose to continue working at a company that offers them less money, relative to a competitor firm, if the organization has a strong culture of belonging. Belonging's impact cannot be understated. It's good for business and, more importantly, for people.

Leaders can develop and strengthen their positivity as well. We train leaders to work through a thirty-day practice of resetting. While any tactics that use these techniques can give you a momentary lift, it is the consistency of daily practice that begins to make changes in one's brain and attitude. Such consistency of cultivation internalizes the practice, so it requires less thought and fewer transitions in one's way of thinking, doing, and being. Our resetting practices include the following:

- **gratitUde**: It is easy to give gratitude to others but can be hard to give to ourselves. The exercise of gratitUde (the capital U forces attention to you in this practice) is to write one thing about yourself for which you are grateful daily for thirty days without any repeats.

- **Post-meeting Positive Takeaway**: We require all meeting participants to write down one positive takeaway at the conclusion of all meetings. Openly sharing them helps to ensure they walk away with an optimistic attitude toward learning and development.
- **Daily Positivity**: We encourage employees to write one positive takeaway from each day. We encourage not only the daily practice but also the weekly review of these positive takeaways to counter negativity bias and build optimism.
- **"I Admire . . ."**: Our secret weapon is to conclude workshops with this exercise. Beyond closing the day on a positive note, it also reminds all the participating leaders why they are doing the important (albeit difficult) work of approaching organizational change and navigating challenges together. Further, it gives each participant something they rarely hear in life and almost never at work: the admiration of a peer. Along with building the individual, research also shows that the art of giving and collectively hearing admiration influences givers, receivers, and witnesses. Such an open exchange makes us more likely to help each other and work together, and improves our attitudes toward our teammates.

Positivity is too often overlooked, and it's something we, as leaders in a tumultuous world that drains our energy, cannot afford to ignore. Cultivating positivity transforms the way we navigate the world and our ability to perform at a peak level, and it makes us more inclined to build bridges and meaningfully connect with others. Positivity is vital for the communities we want to create. It's up to you to use these tools, and we encourage you to lean into this daily practice.

LEARNING FROM LEADERS OF ALL AGES

One privilege of my work is access to so many young people from vastly different life experiences, with amazing gifts and talents. I love being a witness to the early rise of their leadership. Sometimes I even get to be a part of the ways in which they begin to discover themselves and find their way forward. I've had a front-row seat with this with my own children: Ashley, who is an immensely creative and talented entrepreneur, advisor, and leader; and Andrew, a committed student athlete, who began playing team sports at the age of three.

In conducting our research and interviews on leadership, a colleague asked if she could reach out to Andrew to interview him for this book, knowing his experiences of achieving his dream of playing for a Division I team in college—and then walking away from it. I hadn't thought of it, but she was fascinated by his decision to give something up that was a core aspect of his identity. She convinced me that Andrew's story might help to inform and inspire others. I agreed, thinking she might get to 100% of his truth about his experience—always challenging for parents.

Andrew started by telling her, "If you had asked me how I saw myself when I was seven years old, I would have told you that I'm a basketball player." Yet, after years of hard work, early-morning and late-night practices, thousands of miles on road trips—first with his high school team, then as a player with elite traveling teams, and then with the University of Texas basketball team—Andrew Deutser decided to leave the one thing he so closely identified with, basketball, behind. It was a grueling decision that would change his trajectory and force him to consider who he would be going forward. This transition is what former athletes at all levels work through at some point in their lives. It is also what individuals work through as they transition to whatever is next.

"Basketball has always been a part of me. I don't think that will ever change, even though I'm no longer a collegiate player," Andrew told her, adding, "To the people who know me, for the rest of my life, they'll think of me as a basketball player. I'll always have that, even as I add many more accolades and accomplishments to my life, and that is really special to me. I'm proud of everything—the effort, the fight to fit in on team after team with teammates from all over, the mindset I developed to keep pushing through obstacles and to accept my role, to do what everyone said I couldn't, and to achieve the accomplishment to play for a Division I basketball team."

So why did he leave? Andrew found that, after entering college during COVID and having basketball put on hold like thousands of other students, he had become isolated without the connection to the more typical college experience. Basketball and classes, along with campus life, did eventually resume, but Andrew deeply desired a richer experience at the university. He made the decision to give up basketball, the thing that he knew, for the unknown of what would be next. As he describes it, "I knew I wasn't going to become a professional player. I was clear about how amazing it is to be a part of a Division I team—earning my way on as a walk-on player. I had sacrificed many elements of my life and two years of college to achieve my goals and live out my dream. But it came at a price, and I asked myself, is dedicating seven days a week for another two years to basketball worth it in the larger picture of my life? Which am I going to regret more—retiring from basketball with eligibility remaining or not living out my full collegiate experience? I did what was right and best for me."

One thing that played a central role in Andrew's decision was that he wanted to make it himself. He didn't take advice from anyone else and focused on what it would mean to him, his life, his experience. He solicited experiences (not advice) from former athletes, including his mentor and NBA great, T. J. Ford, on how they experienced their own life transitions. But he knew it was his decision and no one else's. He asked himself what he wanted, not what others thought he should do. Of course, there were other factors: a coach leaving UT who he viewed as a mentor and great human, a new coach who Andrew felt didn't appreciate the work done by underplayed team members, graduating friends who would no longer be on the team and who made the road trips more fun. Ultimately, he decided to leave the team, savor the time spent, and acknowledge that it was an accomplishment that to him could last a lifetime.

"I'll always miss being on a team, the fun and excitement of the games, and having that best seat in the house to see the action, but I am 100% satisfied with my decision," Andrew confirms.

Andrew will likely make many more such life-changing decisions, but he'll always remember that he relied on his own leadership on what he most wanted, how he wanted to spend his time and effort, and what he wanted to experience during this phase of his life. He also learned that while he always identified as a basketball player, he now sees himself and the decisions he has made through the eyes of a leader—the leader of himself. I look forward to seeing how he takes this experience forward in life. Sometimes the committed loss of giving up something of great value opens doors that you otherwise would have missed.

ASSESSING THE LEADER OF YOU

By nature, leaders are self-reflective. This doesn't mean that you're meant to linger in the moment, lost in self-reflection during the day's demands. Yet, self-reflection can counteract being reactive and remind you to take needed action to support, modify, or change what you know about yourself.

You have already processed your experiences and life leadership story through the tether exercise. Now it's important to reflect on three areas of leadership:

1. Leader of You
2. Self-Deceptors
3. Belonging Rules Leadership Assessment

Leader of You

In chapter three, we shared the ecosystem model that connects all the elements of a healthy organization. One of these elements is behavioral competencies: expectations we set for every person to individually aspire and work toward. They are also daily habits that we expect employees to live up to and manage effectively. Behavioral competencies are part of how we select, evaluate, interview, coach, and develop people across an organization.

Companies also may have established their own set of leadership competencies. For the Leader of You instrument, however, we have created a set of behavioral competencies that transcend those of an individual organization. Using a competency library that we have cultivated over fifteen years through research and working with leaders, we have identified the thirteen competencies we believe leaders must have and keep developing some level of mastery.

You don't have to be the best in all of them, but invariably there are some that elevate higher than others based on the individual's unique leadership skills. (You'll find more on these competencies in chapter seven and in our institute's teachings.) The Leader of You competencies are as follows:

1. Being Mindful
2. Demonstrating Courage and Grit
3. Recognizing Potential
4. Communicating Effectively
5. Building Relationships
6. Displaying Interpersonal Savvy
7. Learning from Experience
8. Navigating Ambiguity
9. Displaying Creativity
10. Inspiring Others
11. Thinking Strategically
12. Leading Change
13. Positivity

LEADER OF YOU

The **LEADER OF YOU** will help you identify your strengths, weaknesses, and opportunities for improvement.

INSTRUCTIONS: In this exercise, you will review the behavioral competency definitions first and consider how often you exhibit each, marking the frequency on the 1-10 scale. I/O stands for Ineffective use/Overuse. Consider, are there any competencies that you tend to lean in to excessively? Any that you wield ineffectively? If so, mark I/O. When you finish, you'll reflect on your strengths, weaknesses, and areas for growth.

	LEADERSHIP COMPETENCY	Does not exhibit	>	Sometimes exhibits	>	Always exhibits	I/O
PERSONAL	Being Mindful	1 2 3 4 5 6 7 8 9 10					
PERSONAL	Demonstrating Courage + Grit	1 2 3 4 5 6 7 8 9 10					
PERSONAL	Recognizing Potential	1 2 3 4 5 6 7 8 9 10					
SOCIAL	Communicating Effectively	1 2 3 4 5 6 7 8 9 10					
SOCIAL	Building Relationships	1 2 3 4 5 6 7 8 9 10					
SOCIAL	Displaying Interpersonal Savvy	1 2 3 4 5 6 7 8 9 10					
ADAPTABLE	Learning from Experience	1 2 3 4 5 6 7 8 9 10					
ADAPTABLE	Navigating Ambiguity	1 2 3 4 5 6 7 8 9 10					
ADAPTABLE	Displaying Creativity	1 2 3 4 5 6 7 8 9 10					
INTENTIONAL	Inspiring Others	1 2 3 4 5 6 7 8 9 10					
INTENTIONAL	Thinking Strategically	1 2 3 4 5 6 7 8 9 10					
INTENTIONAL	Leading Change	1 2 3 4 5 6 7 8 9 10					
POSITIVITY	Inspiration	1 2 3 4 5 6 7 8 9					
POSITIVITY	Mindfulness	1 2 3 4 5 6 7 8 9					
POSITIVITY	Happiness	1 2 3 4 5 6 7 8 9					
POSITIVITY	Optimism	1 2 3 4 5 6 7 8 9					
POSITIVITY	Gratitude	1 2 3 4 5 6 7 8 9					

Defining Leadership Competencies

Being Mindful
Understands one's own thoughts, feelings, and behaviors and recognizes their impact on others; enhances contribution to the organization by proactively seeking opportunities to develop these skills.

Demonstrating Courage + Grit
Takes initiative and steadfastly mobilizes self to act; demonstrates confidence and candor in difficult situations, gaining support and commitment from others.

Recognizing Potential
Discovers and keeps highly talented employees; makes it a priority to be constantly looking for the next hire.

Communicating Effectively
Cultivates open communication, speaking 100% of the truth; comfortable using a broad range of communication styles, choosing appropriate and effective ways to communicate to different audiences in diverse situations.

Building Relationships
Able to effectively develop mutually beneficial relationships and partnerships based upon trust, respect, and achievement of common goals.

Displaying Interpersonal Savvy
Able to effectively build and grow personal and work relationships; exhibits warmth and approachability, treating people with courtesy and respect; has a way of engaging others that immediately puts people at ease, defusing tense situations.

Learning from Experience
Successfully applies lessons learned from previous experiences to future work; displays a willingness to learn from the past; regularly seeks out feedback from others.

Navigating Ambiguity
Makes sound decisions and achieves forward progress under uncertain circumstances; recognizes what is important and draws on one's knowledge and experience to successfully utilize limited information.

Displaying Creativity
Generates new and unique ideas by making original connections among previously unrelated notions; challenge current ways of thinking; uses unorthodox methods to identify opportunities for improvement in work behaviors and procedures

Inspiring Others
Excites and motivates individuals, teams, or organizations to strive toward a unified vision of the future; demonstrates and ignites passion and purpose; commits to every task with the understanding of each task's larger significance.

Thinking Strategically
Generates and develops unique insights through exploring, evaluating, and integrating information relevant to achieving a goal or set of goals; challenges current ways of thinking.

Leading Change
Establishes and executes the necessary change in a continuously evolving internal and external environment; consistently communicates clear expectations and seeks feedback to successfully navigate the change.

Positivity
A frame of mind that transforms one or more individuals and their organizations through the ability to collectively harness five essential elements—inspiration, mindfulness, happiness, optimism, and gratitude. The continued development and adoption of these five elements as a way of life help to continually manifest productive changes in one's life, and when amplified among other individuals, within an organization.

Identify your top three leadership competencies (i.e., your strengths):

1. _____

2. _____

3. _____

Which two competencies do you need to work on? Write one goal for each.

_____

_____

What leadership competencies do you overuse or ineffectively use? How will you work to resolve this pattern of behavior?

_____

_____

Self-Deceptors

Self-deceptors are the internal forces that can deceive leaders and steer them toward a false narrative, particularly in times of uncertainty, change, or stress. We have identified sixteen deceptors that we find have the most impact on leaders. This does not mean that there aren't other things that deceive you and create false road maps. The ones listed next may jog your awareness of others that act as deceptors to you and your leadership. We want leaders to evaluate each one through two lenses: how often they impact you, and how intensely they impact you and your leadership.

Ego: Makes us more likely to operate in isolation instead of working collaboratively and leaning on others to achieve the best solution. The pride and arrogance that come with ego can increase our odds of exerting excessive control, which impedes our ability to lead with vulnerability.

Smartest in the Room: As leaders, we may feel like others expect us to be right all the time. In response, operating under the guise of "smartest person in the room" syndrome and relying on the need to be right makes us less willing to accept novel ideas and draw on the expertise of team members. We stop listening and become trapped in our own siloed patterns of thinking.

Fitting the Mold: When we feel like leadership needs to look a certain way, or when we don't see ourselves as fitting the leadership mold or a leader image we think we need to live up to, we stop leading from an authentic place and tend to feel like outsiders.

Imposter Syndrome: Feelings of self-doubt can override our ability to make important decisions and act with confidence in leadership positions. When we don't feel up to the challenge due to false notions about our own abilities, we often take the back seat and even sabotage our own success instead of stepping up.

Scarcity: The feeling of never having enough, whether it be time, resources, confidence, or the like, can influence our ability to act and make effective leadership decisions. Scarcity takes us away from issues that require our attention or opportunities that we just don't have the bandwidth for, allowing us to walk away without putting up enough of a fight for things we want and need.

Perfectionism: When everything seems not good enough and we're characterized by a fear of failure that makes every decision feel impossible. Perfectionism causes us to hold on to things too tightly in an effort to keep it all together; we can't let go of control, and strain compulsively and unceasingly toward unattainable goals.

Ambiguity: When we are captive to ambiguity, we exercise control through being vague, not giving the full picture so we retain control, not giving clear direction, or sharing limited or different information with different parties so we're the only one in control of the full picture or story.

Conflict Avoidance: We see conflict as something that will resolve itself. We don't feel the need to lead effectively by intervening. Instead, we defer to everyone else to resolve the issues, agreeing to let things roll over and providing no clear direction. This creates consensus overload.

Busy Barrier: While a leader's time is always in demand, sometimes we hide behind busyness to avoid the "people" side of our role. We become inaccessible and unavailable to rationalize it away because we tell ourselves "we're the boss" and are dealing with things we deem to be more important.

Blame Game: When something goes wrong, it's someone else's fault. We tend to immediately scapegoat others, rather than taking responsibility for our role or being solution oriented.

Situationally Unaware: At times, we may be so absorbed in our own thoughts that we are not tuned into what's really going on. Examples include saying what you want to say, being unable to read the room, preferring to listen to yourself speak, and oversharing or being inappropriate with the information you share.

People Pleasing: In trying to be accepted by others, we minimize our leadership capabilities. We lean too heavily on a desire to live up to

SELF-DECEPTORS

INSTRUCTIONS: Self-deceptors are the internal forces that leaders struggle with that can deceive them and may lead them toward a false narrative, particularly in times of uncertainty, change, or stress.

In this exercise, you can work alone, but we encourage you to work with a trusted colleague, mentor, or coach, someone you think will be honest with you and who will provide you with feedback to enhance your self-awareness.

Reflect on the below list of self-deceptors and corresponding definitions. Then plot using the map how often each deceptor tends to arise for you (i.e., frequency) and the extent to which it impedes you as a leader (i.e., derailment).

If you choose to work with a partner, you will then ask your trusted advisor to fill out the worksheet for you as well. Compare responses once you've both completed the exercise. The reflection questions at the end can spur further dialogue and help you identify potential areas of improvement.

(1) EGO	(5) SCARCITY	(9) BUSY BARRIER	(13) OVER-SIMPLIFICATION
(2) SMARTEST IN THE ROOM	(6) PERFECTIONISM	(10) BLAME GAME	(14) SELECTIVE ETHICS
(3) FITTING THE MOLD	(7) AMBIGUITY	(11) SITUATIONALLY UNAWARE	(15) COMPLIANCE
(4) IMPOSTER SYNDROME	(8) CONFICT AVOIDANCE	(12) PEOPLE PLEASING	(16) BIASES

EGO: Makes us more likely to operate in isolation instead of working collaboratively and leaning on others to achieve the best solution. The pride and arrogance that come with ego can make us more likely to exert excessive control, impeding our ability to lead with vulnerability.

SMARTEST IN THE ROOM: As leaders, we may feel like others expect us to be right all the time, but operating under the guise of "smartest person in the room" syndrome and relying on the need to be right make us less willing to accept novel ideas and draw on the expertise of team members. We stop listening and become trapped in our own siloed patterns of thinking.

FITTING THE MOLD: When we feel like leadership needs to look a certain way or when we don't see ourselves as fitting the leadership image. We think we need to live up to that image, we stop leading from an authentic place, and we tend to feel like outsiders.

IMPOSTER SYNDROME: Feelings of self-doubt can override our ability to make important decisions and act with confidence in leadership positions. When we don't feel up to the challenge due to false notions about our own abilities, we often take the back seat and may even sabotage our own success instead of stepping up to the plate.

SCARCITY: The feeling of never having enough, whether it be time, resources, confidence, etc., can influence our ability to act and make effective leadership decisions, taking us away from issues that require our attention and allowing us to walk away without putting up enough of a fight.

PERFECTIONISM: When everything is not good enough and we're characterized by a fear of failure, making every decision feel impossible; trying to hold things too tightly and keep it all together; can't let go of control; straining compulsively and unceasingly toward unattainable goals.

AMBIGUITY: Control through being vague, not giving the full picture so you have control, not giving clear direction, sharing limited information or different info to different parties so you're the only one in control of the full story; controlling the flow of information.

CONFLICT AVOIDANCE: Sees conflict as something that will resolve itself; doesn't feel the need to intervene and defers to everyone else to resolve the issues instead of effectively leading. Agrees to let things roll over and provides no clear direction, creating consensus overload.

BUSY BARRIER: While a leader's time is always in demand, sometimes we hide behind "busyness" to avoid the "people side" of our role. We become inaccessible and unavailable to rationalize it away because we tell ourselves "we're the boss" and are dealing with things we deem more important.

BLAME GAME: When something goes wrong, it's someone else's fault. We tend to immediately scapegoat others, rather than taking responsibility for our role or being solution oriented.

SITUATIONALLY UNAWARE: At times we may be so absorbed in our own thoughts that we are not tuned in to what's really going on. Examples include saying what you want to say, an inability to read the room, liking to listen to yourself speak, oversharing and being inappropriate with the information you share.

PEOPLE PLEASING: In trying to be accepted by others you minimize your leadership capabilities, leaning too heavily on a desire to live up to people's expectations and appeasing the group instead of doing what you know is right.

OVER-SIMPLIFICATION: It's black or it's white, good or bad; there's no nuance and no middle ground. This deceptor makes us want to give overly simplistic responses to put ourselves and others at ease even when the situation calls for greater discussion and the need to pause to navigate complexity.

SELECTIVE ETHICS: When we act in ways that are inconsistent with our personal values or ethics but choose to ignore this fact, hiding it from ourselves and others because it serves us in some way.

COMPLIANCE: Doing something to complete it, to "check the box," rather than taking the time to effectively solve the problem and approach something with a committed mindset.

BIASES: Notions and assumptions about how people should behave and how they do behave. Our biases are characterized by preconceptions, stereotypes, and prejudices, making us more likely to favor or dismiss certain people or ideas.

REFLECTION:

1. Which deceptors stand out as ones you need to be more aware of and work on in your day-to-day interactions? What cues will you introduce in your routine to enhance self-awareness?

_____

_____

2. How will you reveal these deceptors to others? How will you foster greater awareness in your organization so people aren't as hindered by these negative forces?

_____

_____

3. How does overreliance on any of the deceptors derail efforts to foster belonging?

_____

_____

people's expectations and appease the group instead of doing what we know is right.

Oversimplification: Things are always black or white, good or bad; there's no nuance and no middle ground. We tend to give overly simplistic responses to put ourselves and others at ease, and because we have a binary bias (seeing a simple yes or no, A or B), even when the situation calls for greater discussion and the need to pause to navigate complexity.

Selective Ethics: We fall prey to this deceptor when we act in ways that are inconsistent with our personal values or ethics but choose to ignore this fact, hiding it from ourselves and others because it serves us in some way.

Compliance: When we do something just to complete it, to "check the box," rather than taking the time to approach something with a committed mindset and effectively solve the problem.

Biases: When we possess notions and assumptions about how people should and do behave. Our biases are characterized by preconceptions, stereotypes, and prejudices that make us more likely to favor or dismiss certain people or ideas.

Belonging Leadership Essentials

At the heart of belonging is personal fit. Many leaders fear to ask the right question—not *where* do I fit, but rather, *do* I fit? Those shaped by deeply embedded organizational structures are often too quick to answer the question of whether a leader fits, even the strongest, most tenured leaders. Yet, it is not the organization's answer on which we rely, but our own. You decide your fit. You decide when and what to fight for and how you can best make an impact.

Even seasoned leaders have been surprised at how radically their results have changed when they became intentional about belonging. When we are centered in our own identity and capacity for contribution, the ability to challenge everything becomes a reliable tool. As we think about our fit and our place in the belonging equation, we can determine what must be redesigned, reoriented, and repurposed for our ability to navigate today's challenges.

Leaders are required to assemble diverse teams; understand their strengths and weaknesses; empathize with and solicit nuanced, diverse perspectives; and sustain positive, enduring relationships, all while advancing the organization's bottom line. The superhuman stamina and foresight being demanded of leaders under constant threat of making a misstep detracts from the boldness required to bring people together effectively and meaningfully elevate their contributions.

The belonging leader understands the unique, constantly evolving, sometimes elusive opportunity that each day presents them. They can deftly navigate between those who have and do not have, those who care and do not care, those who see the whole and those who see only a part. They tackle the complicated work of creating equilibrium as they listen, design, create, and implement change. One of the greatest challenges of the belonging leader is not whether to change or determine the ultimate solution; rather, it is the speed at which to implement change, and how the leader chooses to explain their vision for it.

Yes, the belonging leader is expected to show off their superpowers. And when they happen to encounter their personal kryptonite, and they are at their most challenged, exhausted, and threatened, all eyes will be on them and how they choose. It is in these moments where the belonging leader is defined: Will they be open to creating solutions and spaces that bring others into their leadership, or will they shrink their circle to exclude and elevate only those closest to them?

The leader-of-you framing helps build the emotional intelligence and cultural competence that belonging leaders require. Beyond that, to create cultures of acceptance and unity, belonging leaders need to engage deeply with each of the five Belonging Rules, understanding what they are and how to live them out day to day. Belonging leadership is about behaving in ways that align with your identity, promoting a collective experience of "we're all in this together" and "we're all safe here," while giving people the fuel so desperately needed to perform at the highest level.

The following list describes actions that leaders can start taking to reinforce and uphold the five rules in their organizations, the summation of which along with the leader of you helps to infuse belonging.

- **Turning in to the power** necessitates that leaders be prepared to listen to and learn from any individual in the organization who speaks up in the pursuit of fairness, equity, and inclusion. Leaders must assess the structures that preserve inequities and the biases and behaviors that lead to exclusion. They also need to understand how the landscape of their organization perpetuates behaviors and actions inconsistent with the leader's vision of what is necessary and right and must be willing to act in ways that defy the status quo such that appropriate and meaningful change for that organization can be pursued and enacted.

- **Listening without labels** is crucial for fostering open yet challenging environments, ones where differences are engaged and celebrated rather than hidden or disregarded. Listening without labels involves listening from the heart, from a place of curiosity and no judgment. It requires attention to stereotypes and bias (as noted earlier, we are hardwired to engage from a place of craving similarity versus celebrating differences). This type of listening empowers us to get to the root of every issue, to engage one another with curiosity and steer clear of quick, prescriptive judgments. Leaders who master this rule hear what is spoken without judgment while engaging the unspoken with humanity and heart. They adjust and adapt to all different cultures, values, and perspectives.

- **Empowering identity over purpose** requires an accurate and authentic evaluation of the organization as well as all individuals within it. Leaders need to recognize and be able to discuss identities in all their complexity and wholeness. They need to understand identity as the organization's ecosystem and all the elements within it. By recognizing the complexity of organizational identity, leaders can better understand how to celebrate difference and reap the rewards of diversity instead of forcing assimilation or inauthenticity. Belonging leaders know that the organizational identity can be evolved, so they regularly question its assumptions to ensure all employees feel like they belong to a common purpose, something worth aligning their individual selves with.

- **Challenging everything** rests upon the creation of a psychologically safe environment, one where everyone feels secure in speaking up, be it with positive or critical feedback. Leaders who challenge everything welcome critical conversations, drawing on effective challenges to see them through. By embedding this rule, belonging leaders create cultures of creativity, as speaking up and out becomes the norm at all levels, rather than a suggestion or, at worst, a violation. Leaders can develop and encourage greater challenge from all organizational members by encouraging speech and dissent while ensuring that personal attacks or any form of discrimination will not be tolerated. Leaders should continuously engage in employee listening, prioritizing collaborative discussions where employees are afforded ample opportunity to speak up and out.

- **Leaders who give and receive 100% of the truth** develop radically transparent and trusting organizational cultures, creating the space for belonging by ensuring

BELONGING RULES
LEADERSHIP SURVEY

Discover how strong of a belonging leader you are.

INSTRUCTIONS: If you'd like to take the "Belonging Rules" survey and receive a personalized insights report to foster belonging in your organization, please aim your phone camera at the below QR code. You'll be asked to share your email, and we'll share recommendations and insights on where you stand.

that mutual respect and difficult conversations go hand in hand. Encouraging 100% of the truth does not allow for an atmosphere of disrespect or aggression, but it does call for trust, self-awareness, empathy, humility, and honesty. Leaders continuously seek improvement on belonging by garnering honest feedback from both internal and external stakeholders, working to create environments that encourage authentic connection.

BREAKTHROUGH LEADERSHIP

As I think about leaders who embody this framework and live out the Belonging Rules in their daily actions and interactions, I think of the University of Arizona football team's head coach, Jedd Fisch. I have known Coach Fisch for nearly two decades. I have been with him at his happiest moments and his lowest moments, like when he had an aortic aneurysm that almost took his life at twenty-six years of age. He has exhibited an all-too-rare form of leadership and perseverance. In addition to overcoming a life-threatening health issue, he had been overlooked for promotions and head-coaching opportunities. Yet, he was undeterred. He truly embraced being the leader of his own life and destiny. He spent time working on himself as a leader in our Institute, making sure he was growing outside football while being prepared to lead when he did get the opportunity.

Few coaches have Jedd's pedigree. He has worked for coaches Bill Belichick, Sean McVay, Pete Carroll, Jim Harbaugh, Mike Shanahan, Steve Spurrier, and Brian Billick, just to name a few. He was the fruit of many coaching trees, most stemming from the sport's most frequent winners and from Super Bowl champions and Hall of Famers.

Yet, when he finally got his chance to become a head coach, it came with a challenge: turning around a program in decline. The University of Arizona had not won a football game for 763 days. The program was spiraling to the lowest levels of the NCAA, with one of the worst recruiting rankings and a football facility in total disrepair

The university understood during the selection process that the turnaround would be too big for someone who had simply won at other places. They were in search of a brilliant tactician, someone who could bring a philosophy and approach. They needed someone who had overcome real challenges, disappointments, and setbacks on and off the field; someone who would not give in to the status quo or the false belief that Arizona was only a basketball school—albeit a great one. They were also looking for a leader of character, one who could intentionally connect the dots that were disconnected across the program—culture, facility, players, recruits, coaches, staff, donors, fans, alumni, former players, community—and build a program that could literally and figuratively withstand the desert heat. They were looking for Jedd Fisch.

Still, the new coach was unproven as a head coach and offered no flashy profile for the hungry fanbase. Jedd's objective was to create energy, turn this desperate program around, bring people back into the Wildcat fanbase, and create hope. He knew that his mission was to convince everyone not only that he was right but also that he could inspire change and win the right way. Jedd felt the pressure from day one.

The pressure from alumni and Arizona's dwindling fanbase to press forward with a proven coach immediately conflicted with the University's decision to affect systemic and sustainable change with Coach Fisch. Football fans are known to rally around the battle cry of traditional coach-speak like, "We are going to rebuild from the ground up" and "It'll take time and patience." When, instead, the new motto chosen was "It's personal"—a message aimed at humanizing the new coach, his program, and his off-field development focus and culture change initiative—the fanbase did just that and began to take their program personally. The aggressiveness and deeply personal nature of the message, tied with the actions of a new coach—including presenting a visual plan for a redesigned facility and player experience—made this motto tangible, real, and, yes, personal.

Nike picked up the "It's personal" messaging within twenty-four hours of its release and made it viral. Back in Arizona, as part of making it personal, Coach Fisch worked to humanize himself, not as a coach but as someone who cared deeply about doing things the right way—his way—the new Wildcat Way. Jedd created the only facility and program of its kind in the NCAA, a Leadership Learning Lab called the 5th Quarter, to develop every player and the leader within each player for the rest of their lives. The facility, patterned after our Clarity Institute, was a game changer, as people began to see just how much he cared about the human under the helmet.

Coach Fisch had started the epic turnaround, knowing that the first year would be year zero of a five-year rebuild. His end goal seemed so far away and he felt he was on the right track. Then the season started.

When college football coaches laboring mightily to win measure success on only 9 days out of 365, every loss takes an unappreciated toll. Yet, through loss after loss, through injured players (including his top three quarterbacks), through hurtful diatribes directed at him and his family in the community, Jedd stayed true to his plan, to his belief in a different future state, and to a path he was committed to carving—one where, as Coach said, "there are no rules, only values." This path included a major, highly original redesign of every space and room in the football facility to invite people back into the program and create a shared vision for its future.

As a result, in a few short months, Coach Fisch was able to do what no one (except the university president and athletic department leadership) believed possible. He started turning the giant program around and creating a space where everyone started to believe and feel like they belonged to something with great potential for success.

He included coaches in culture-forming exercises (marking the first time in their careers when they had been invited into the conversation);

developed the Wildcat Way with defined values, behaviors, and what it means to be a PRO (Purposeful, Resilient, and Original); dramatically increased social media impressions; and raised millions of dollars for the facility redesign and student athlete development. Coach Fisch recruited the twenty-sixth-highest-ranked incoming freshman class in the country, exceeded season ticket goals, and stopped the 763-day losing streak by beating the University of California for the team's first win. He resuscitated the program in less than twelve months and created space where alumni, existing students, and new enrollees, formerly uninterested in a losing team, could belong as Wildcat fans.

Coach Fisch made this program personal for everyone. In fact, you'll find that motto as a visual reminder on the front of *The Wildcat Way* (a printed book for every student athlete), on T-shirts and practice shorts, affixed to every machine in the redesigned weight room, painted in graphics on the ceiling as players enter the field, on flags, and in the locker room. Everywhere a player could be, they were reminded to take every effort, every defeat and victory, every contribution and make it personal. And, as Jedd has shown with his personal commitment to the players and the university, they continue to win. His second season was marked by five wins—exceeding everyone's expectation, except his own.

WHERE BELONGING BEGINS

The leader of you requires constant reappraisal and recalibration. It's about understanding your identity and your innate leadership qualities, the factors in your environment that advance or constrain you, and the crucial leadership behaviors necessary for inspiring belonging. By focusing on your unique leadership stories and the perspective through which you see the world, you can start to open up to others, learning from and incorporating the concepts of belonging—including ensuring a diverse environment—in a more intentional way.

Chapter 7

THE BOX OF BELONGING

FRAMING YOUR LEADERSHIP

A t Deutser, we think about belonging as a space. But, as such, it can be hard to conceptualize. At times it is palpable; other times it is vague and undefined. Yet, when we create literal physical space that fosters togetherness and openness, we also work to create figurative space where those same connections can take root and flourish.

When we interview and study people to determine what belonging means to them, many describe a type of understanding where you have full acceptance—a feeling, a mindset—that you know and can feel when you have it. While that may be true, we have worked to provide more clearly delineated boundaries and identify specific behavioral competencies that help leaders understand how to think through what makes up their Box of Belonging.

Deutser created the Box of Belonging framework to unpack and explore who we are as leaders. Throughout this chapter, we will dive deeply into the framework of the box and define each of the four sides. By understanding your relationship with each side, you can begin to construct your box, paving the way for belonging to emerge. The box offers us the ability to see ourselves through a series of leadership competencies. Further, breaking the box down into individual components enables us to look at ourselves openly and honestly. When we don't stop to evaluate ourselves through a truthful lens and recognize the biases that influence us, we potentially become reactive and veer from our intentional path of fostering belonging for others in organizations.

The box of belonging gives us a way to contextualize and frame how we experience leadership and effectively bring diverse groups of people into our spaces so everyone feels enjoyed, supported, and accepted. This framework also helps us identify where there is misalignment between our leadership priorities and competencies and, ultimately, discover fit for ourselves and others.

ORIGINS OF THE BOX

For multiple decades, my company has studied human performance. Our results show that performance, creativity, and innovation emanate from a defined framework. This is true of some of the world's top performers. Think about theater and the constraints of the stage, or athletes and the size of their field, pitch, or court. I first realized the value of frameworks while working for Ringling Bros. and Barnum & Bailey Circus. I was mesmerized by the space created within the three rings. I was struck by the focus that a simple structure provided the performers as well as the audience. A whole world was taking place in each ring, yet they all coexisted. This new awareness informed my thinking about defined spaces and their impact on performance, eventually inspiring me to study the concept extensively. It became my grounding principle for leadership and organizational frameworks.

"Thinking outside the box" sounds like a great way to spur creativity and innovation, but it can take you in directions far removed from your true goals or potential. We have observed that thinking outside the box creates greater confusion because on the outside there are no boundaries and too many variables. There are too many unknowns. Instead, leaders and organizations have a much better chance of success when they understand the parameters they're working *within*, then work from there to stretch the box to meet their goals and vision. In other words, identifying and acknowledging real-world limitations can actually help to spark creativity by facilitating focus, rather than using an open-ended, "anything goes" approach that doesn't reliably result in ideas that can be practically implemented.

While thinking outside the box offers the allure of freedom without constraint, thinking inside the box gives you structure and an approach to thoughtful expansion, providing a foundational springboard. Leaders conditioned to an "outside-the-box thinking" mentality may find this logic counterintuitive. But real-world results of using their long-held ideal to enhance creativity and performance fall short. Our research shows that defining the box is fundamental to sustained success for the leader and the organization: it tells leaders where to lead from and people in an organization where they belong. The definition is important. It is a similar principle to how we teach children to color within the lines and play in the sandbox with others.

Truly, most successful leaders and organizations operate from *within* their defined box, because it provides the leader the control necessary to purposefully navigate the inherent change in an environment and carefully connect employees to the things that matter most. Leaders that understand the intricacies of their box are able to unlock the organizational DNA that makes possible enduring, sustainable replication and growth.

When you work within the box, your playing field is better defined and you have greater understanding of specifics and their possible impact. This improved clarity increases the empathy and connectivity in the box. The box perspective is critical not only for the leader when defining the parameters of the organization but also for the employees as they work to understand the business goals and elements that directly impact them. Further, the box provides a critical context for the board and leader when working together to create commonality around the expectations of the company.

I pride myself on being an innovator; however, admittedly, I don't always innovate with discipline. I am at my best and my solutions are best when I have the focus to stay within my defined boundaries, pushing innovation to the far reaches of the box. So, as you begin to think about your box, think not about where you fit, either inside or outside. Instead, ask the right question: Is your box sized appropriately for you? Then the next question, that of fit, becomes much easier to answer.

One of the most impactful pieces of art in our offices is a frame with many old and used paint cans, all different sizes, shapes, and colors, each bashed up in their own way. Now, many people would say this is trash—and without the frame and structure, that's exactly what it is. But within the frame—the box—the cans tell a brilliant story that encapsulates not only our work but the concept of belonging. Each unique can is united by what they have in common. While the brilliance of the art may appear to be the uniqueness of the cans, they are nothing without the value of the frame holding them together to create art.

The powerful point is that the box is of your own making. There are no rules or regulations with the box, and no size requirement—only you can determine the right box for your leadership. You get to construct one that is big enough for your wildest performance objectives, while allowing enough focus to achieve the goals you establish. And understand that while the sides of the box exist, they can be permeable (letting things flow in and out) and flexible (expanding or contracting when necessary)—but once you let something inside, it interacts with the whole. Think of the three rings of the circus operating under the big-top tent. Everything happens within a defined ecosphere of your choosing and creation. How you define your box, and how willing you are to push the parameters inside it, are critical to sustaining your long-term performance.

THE BOX OF BELONGING

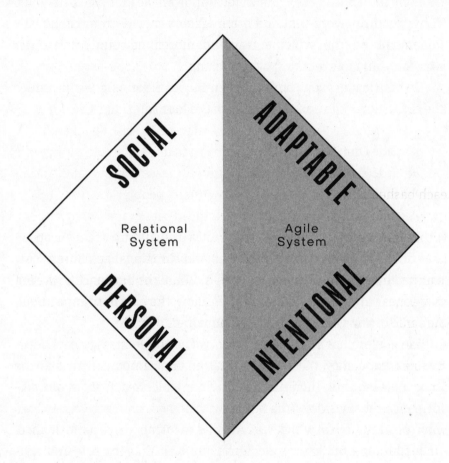

SOCIAL

ADAPTABLE

Relational System

Agile System

PERSONAL

INTENTIONAL

BUILDING YOUR BOX

The most successful leaders we work with create their framework by using the Box of Belonging as their mental model and building its sides through the construct of the most important leadership behaviors. This structure gives them and other leaders they encounter the best understanding from which to lead and, more importantly, gives their workforce and followers a space to belong.

To help leaders start building their Box of Belonging, we introduce the construct of the box, starting with the four sides:

- Side One: Personal
- Side Two: Social
- Side Three: Adaptable
- Side Four: Intentional

Each side has distinct definitions and functional measures. How leaders intentionally construct each side and understand how each integrates with the whole framework allows for more informed decision making and, ultimately, better outcomes.

We explore not only the definitions and uniqueness of each leadership competency, but also the relationships among them and the impact each has on the others. We do not look for deficits in our performance on any side of the box or with any competency. Instead, we look for strengths on which we can build to further drive performance. Understanding the key connection points within each side and relative to each competency is essential to our ability to evolve and grow as leaders.

Side One: The Personal Side of the Box

This side takes a strong personal inventory of your impact on others and increases your awareness of how you show up to contribute to your own life, the lives of those around you, and to your organization. As a leader, your first priority is to effectively lead yourself, and, as an extension of that competency, to lead your teams, which can be your family, your volunteer group, a special project, and your company.

This side of the box addresses three competencies that help to frame our personal approach to leadership: being mindful, demonstrating courage and grit, and recognizing potential.

Being Mindful: Our brand of mindfulness focuses on understanding your place and creating space to allow for originality, equanimity, and increased energy flow. We look at motivations, personal strengths and limitations, and emotions.

Demonstrating Courage and Grit: We examine ways to stay true to your vision and values by standing up for your convictions in the face of opposition while working to proactively gain support and commitment from others.

Recognizing Potential: We explore ways to enhance our ability to "see" those around us and activate their best. We explore your willingness to bring in people from outside of your personal comfort zone, ensuring a diversity of backgrounds and opinions while introducing a challenge to identify personal bias.

Side Two: The Social Side of the Box

There is enormous power in our relationships. At any given time, we are either building, repairing, or advancing relationships. Where we are on that continuum often relies on elements of trust and accountability.

This side of the box addresses three competencies that most influence and define our social competencies: communicating effectively, building relationships, and displaying interpersonal savvy.

Communicating Effectively: This competency sets the tone for, and becomes the cadence of, your leadership style. We cultivate open communication that anchors to trust building, is positive and human centered, and is designed on the platform of speaking 100% of the truth.

Building Relationships: Being able to effectively develop relationships built on the Belonging Rules creates partnerships based on understanding, trust, open and honest discourse, respect, and achievement of common goals. This competency recalibrates human connection (making people real) with other business goals and imperatives.

Displaying Interpersonal Savvy: Here we take a fresh look at recognizing your own emotions, thoughts, and feelings to better understand how these impact others. We teach how to effectively defuse tense situations and resolve conflict through tact, diplomacy, and solution design, all of which contribute to expanding the scope of belonging. Proficiency in these skills tears down the picket fences that block inclusion and resolution.

Side Three: The Adaptable Side of the Box

A leader who cultivates belonging excels in adaptability. Here we focus on the leadership competencies that drive us to work in a perpetual state of graceful and fluent recalibration.

This side of the box addresses three competencies that influence and dictate our ability to be adaptable: learning from experience, navigating ambiguity, and displaying creativity.

Learning from Experience: Making intentional adjustments by applying what is learned from previous experiences shows a willingness to remain open without rigidity or attachment to what you've known to be true in the past. When we are open to past experiences, we can increase our capacity to understand and expand space for others.

Navigating Ambiguity: Leaders must become adept at recognizing what is important to focus on while successfully working with limited, emerging, uncertain, or missing information. The velocity of change and the increasing numbers of inputs elevate the uncertainty of the environments where we operate. Successfully navigating ambiguity is one of the leadership qualities most aligned with sustainable forward movement.

Displaying Creativity: Leaders must challenge current ways of thinking that lessen our inhibitions and worn pathways, with the goal of opening us up for fresh approaches. The adaptable leader accepts that displaying creativity is in fact innovation, even in the form of communication, organizational design, finance, problem solving, space utilization, or human interaction. Creativity doesn't always have to look or feel creative—rather, it is the energy that brings new possibility.

Side Four: The Intentional Side of the Box

Intentionality is fundamental to great leadership and followership. Here we focus on the competencies that ensure a purposeful pathway forward and challenge the more improvisational approaches that leaders take.

This side of the box addresses three competencies that most influence and help to determine our intentionality: inspiring others, thinking strategically, and leading change.

Inspiring Others: In order to lead, someone must follow. Leaders may struggle when working through this competency, as they believe it is either an inherent quality or they have previously neither understood nor experienced the human element of their inspiration. This competency helps us to live and operate in a way that demonstrates and ignites both a passion and purpose that move others to action.

Thinking Strategically: Leaders often overly complicate strategy, but we define strategy simply as "the definition of a desired change." Critical to strategy is the willingness to forgo the expected response for the more strategic one, giving way to increased inclusion of ideas, circumstances, and people. Leaders must work to identify new pathways to strategic development that better serve the acceleration of change in the business environment and acknowledge the pull of emerging influences.

Leading Change: While this seems like an obvious aspect of leadership, it has risen to become leaders' most urgent competency demand, given the speed of change today and the bombardment of factors influencing it. This one area touches on the need for calibration across the previous eleven competencies making up the four sides of the Box of Belonging. We are often part of change or require change of others, but in either case, leading through change requires an advanced skillset.

Our World Is Multidimensional

Interestingly, the box isn't flat and two-dimensional, with only four sides. Rather, it is a three-dimensional cube, a more complex framework akin to the multidimensional problems modern leaders face. This requires a different understanding of dimensionality throughout the company and in your leadership.

While we don't place a hierarchy of importance on any sides of the box, we have experienced transformational moments with our clients when they have begun by focusing on the bottom side—*organizational identity*. It focuses on key elements from chapter three, such as characteristics, purpose, values, behaviors, and traditions, which together form the foundation upon which everything else rests. Leaders often believe they have addressed these elements, yet employees yearn deeply for greater definition. The most effective leaders understand the importance of defining these elements for themselves and their organizations.

The top of the box, *environmental factors*, represents your window into the world, serving as your funnel connecting to all the external forces and extending to all your personal and organizational stakeholders. This side requires a different lens into the surrounding environment, including industry evolution and the competitive landscape, which are inextricably linked to the internal environmental factors. These factors in turn provide understanding of the world around us so we can align with it to create the consistency and transparency crucial to building trust.

The following exercises encourage thoughtful self-reflection—you will delve deeply into the personal, social, adaptable, and intentional sides of the box by responding to a series of open-ended questions. In building out all four sides, you begin to understand how you approach and embody belonging leadership. We're all different—with our own unique opportunities to grow. I find these exercises are like looking in a mirror—they force you as a leader to recognize your blind spots and the areas where you may need to intentionally challenge yourself to achieve the growth necessary to foster belonging in the organizations you lead.

Instructions: In this exercise, you'll take a look in the mirror. We want you to reflect on each of the leadership competencies—the personal, social, adaptable, and intentional sides of the box—and use the questions below to conduct a thorough self-reflection. This will help you begin to understand yourself as a leader and your impact on others.

PERSONAL
UNDERSTANDING YOURSELF

BEING MINDFUL

RECOGNIZING POTENTIAL

How do I impact those around me?

DEMONSTRATING COURAGE + GRIT

BEING MINDFUL

Understands one's own thoughts, feelings, and behaviors and recognizes their impact on others; enhances contribution to the organization by proactively seeking opportunities to develop these skills.

· What does it feel like to be mindful?

_____

· When do you find yourself being mindful the most?

_____

· Who in my life demonstrates being mindful? How?

_____

· Are there times when I have chosen not to be mindful?

_____

· How could you improve being mindful?

_____

DEMONSTRATING COURAGE + GRIT

Takes initiative and steadfastly mobilizes self to act; demonstrates confidence and candor in difficult situations, gaining support and commitment from others.

· Who are some leaders you know who demonstrate courage and grit?

_____

· What do courage and grit look like in your life?

_____

· When was the most recent time that you exhibited courage and grit?

_____

· When is a time you failed to demonstrate courage and grit?

_____

· What can you do to develop your ability to have courage and show grit?

_____

RECOGNIZING POTENTIAL

Discovers and motivates highly dedicated teammates; makes it a priority to be constantly supportive and encourage growth.

· How do you recognize potential in yourself?

_____

· How do you recognize potential in others?

_____

· What do you do once you recognize potential in someone?

_____

· In what ways can you access your untapped potential?

_____

· What can you do to help someone unlock their full potential?

_____

SOCIAL
MAKING CONNECTIONS

COMMUNICATING EFFECTIVELY

BUILDING RELATIONSHIPS

Are you having meaningful interactions with people?

DISPLAYING INTERPERSONAL SAVVY

COMMUNICATES EFFECTIVELY

Creates open communication, speaking 100% of the truth; comfortable using a broad range of communication styles; works to actively listen.

· In what ways are you an effective communicator?

_____

· What do you enjoy most about communicating with others?

_____

· What can you do to improve your communication?

_____

· What leader in history was a great communicator? Why?

_____

· How do you know when you have effectively communicated?

_____

BUILDING RELATIONSHIPS

Able to effectively develop mutually beneficial relationships and partnerships based upon trust, respect, and achievement of common goals.

· What does a "meaningful relationship" look like to you?

_____

· In what ways can you work toward having deeper interactions with your teammates?

_____

· What is inhibiting your ability to build meaningful relationships with others?

_____

· Describe a time when you needed to repair a relationship. How did you do it?

_____

· Are there any patterns to how your relationships end?

_____

DISPLAYING INTERPERSONAL SAVVY

Able to effectively build and grow personal and professional relationships; exhibits warmth and approachability, treating people with courtesy and respect; has a way of engaging others that immediately puts people at ease, defusing tense situations; understands the environment.

· How well do you display interpersonal savvy?

_____

· How could you improve displaying interpersonal savvy?

_____

· Who in your life displays effective interpersonal savvy?

_____

Do you make a conscious effort to recognize how others feel when they are around you?

_____

What can you do to be more consistent in displaying interpersonal savvy?

_____

Instructions: In this exercise, you'll take a look in the mirror. We want you to reflect on each of the leadership competencies—the personal, social, adaptable, and intentional sides of the box—and use the questions below to conduct a thorough self-reflection. This will help you begin to understand yourself as a leader and your impact on others.

ADAPTABLE

RESPONDING TO THE ENVIRONMENT

LEARNING FROM EXPERIENCE

DISPLAYING CREATIVITY

How do you utilize your experience in daily life?

NAVIGATING AMBIGUITY

LEARNING FROM EXPERIENCE

Successfully applies lessons learned from previous experiences to future work; displays a willingness to learn from the past; regularly seeks out feedback from others.

· Do you slow down and actively learn from past experiences?

_____

· Are you effective at applying what you learn from your experiences?

_____

· What was an experience you learned from?

_____

· Were you able to apply your learning to another situation?

_____

· Do you learn more from your successes or failures?

_____

NAVIGATING AMBIGUITY

Makes sound decisions and achieves forward progress under uncertain circumstances;
recognizes what is important and draws on one's knowledge and experience to successfully
utilize limited information.

· Is an ambiguous circumstance negative, positive, or a mix of both?

_____

· How often are you in circumstances with limited information or direction?

_____

· How do you deal with uncertainty?

_____

· What contributes to the ambiguity you face in your life?

_____

· What is the best outcome when you've dealt with an ambiguous situation?

_____

DISPLAYING CREATIVITY

Generates new and unique ideas by making original connections among previously unrelated
notions; challenges current ways of thinking; uses unorthodox methods to identify opportunities
for improvement in work behaviors and procedures.

· How do you display creativity?

_____

· Describe a time when you displayed creativity.

_____

· What are different types of creativity you use?

_____

· Where do you find you are most creative?

_____

· Does creativity come naturally to you, or do you have to work at it?

_____

· How can you increase your creativity in solving problems?

_____

Instructions: In this exercise, you'll take a look in the mirror. We want you to reflect on each of the leadership competencies—the personal, social, adaptable, and intentional sides of the box—and use the questions below to conduct a thorough self-reflection. This will help you begin to understand yourself as a leader and your impact on others.

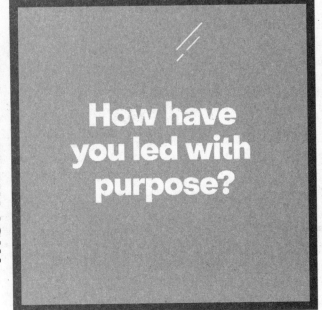

INTENTIONAL
PURPOSEFUL ACTION

INSPIRING OTHERS

LEADING CHANGE

How have you led with purpose?

THINKING STRATEGICALLY

INSPIRING OTHERS

Excites and motivates individuals, teams, or organizations; demonstrates and ignites passion and purpose.

· What does it mean to inspire others?

_____

· How does it make you feel when you inspire others?

_____

· Who inspires you?

_____

· What can you do to be more inspirational?

_____

· Can you describe a time you inspired someone else to achieve success?

_____

THINKING STRATEGICALLY

Generates and develops unique insights through exploring, evaluating, and integrating information relevant to achieving a goal or set of goals; challenges current ways of thinking.

· How often do you think strategically?

_____

· What role does strategic thinking play in your daily work?

_____

· How could you improve as a strategic thinker?

_____

· Who is the best strategic thinker you know, and what makes them great?

_____

· Can you describe a time when your strategic thinking led to a major accomplishment?

_____

LEADING CHANGE

Establishes and executes the necessary change in a continuously evolving environment; consistently communicates clear expectations and seeks feedback to successfully navigate the change.

· When were you put in charge of leading change?

_____

· What did you do to get people to follow?

_____

· What challenges did you face trying to create change?

_____

· What is one thing you would do differently next time you lead change?

_____

· Do you see change as a positive or negative in your life?

_____

MAKING SENSE OF THE SIDES

As we continue to reflect upon the connections across the box, we explore the relationships within each side as well as among them. We also look at the broader framing of the box through two distinct but related systems: the Relational and the Agile. Each system is considered in its totality. The Relational System comprises the Personal and Social sides of the box, and the Agile System comprises the Adaptable and Intentional sides. Each system tells a unique story, so leaders need to understand their interplay.

Belonging-focused leaders understand the importance of creating balance among the Relational and Agile systems. The systems need to be balanced to create the necessary and healthy flow of energy, ideas, and leadership within a leader and their organization. Identifying areas of balance versus imbalance begins with a thorough examination of each side of the box. When we consider the Agile system on its own, we're addressing the constancy and relentlessness of change while also exploring the concept of leading change from an identity-driven, intentional lens. Organizational environments are rife with conflict, tension, and ambiguity, not to mention new and unique relationships leaders must constantly manage and sustain. Leaders therefore cannot wade through change without a plan. The best leaders view change through a scientific and strategic mindset. They experiment, testing alternative approaches to come to better and more inclusive solutions. When considering change, they always keep belonging in mind, ensuring that their actions align with their values such that all change-oriented decisions continue to empower, engage, and unify the people they impact.

That said, the Agile system cannot be fully actualized without leaning into the Relational system. This is because we cannot lead change, or lead with intentionality, without understanding how we see ourselves, how we see others, and how others see us. Leaders need to bring together people of all different backgrounds, in all different functions, to deliver optimal outcomes and navigate volatile, uncertain, complex, and ambiguous landscapes. The Relational system involves how we think about ourselves and interact with others. These internal and external components of self-awareness jointly influence our success as leaders. To instill belonging, leaders need to cultivate meaningful, positive relationships with all group members and foster inclusive environments that encourage knowledge sharing, collaboration, flourishing, and development. As leaders pursue a journey toward belonging-focused and inclusive leadership, they need to be mindful of their own strengths, weaknesses, and the times when they are less likely to show up as their most effective selves.

Many leaders will subconsciously favor one system over the other. Even exceptional leaders are rarely in exact balance. This is not an intentional choice; it is often a matter of where their strengths more naturally lie. Too many leaders spend unnecessary time on where they perform the lowest. This is a loser's game that forces decisions with the potential to distract you from being the best you. Instead, identify where you have the greatest opportunity for growth—say, by accentuating a strength, closing a gap, or addressing a weakness. Core to our teaching is to make sure that leaders do not obsess over their weaknesses and put all their energy there. Before you make decisions on which area to attack first, step back and look at the big picture. Also, be aware that sometimes you can actually overprioritize your strengths, which covers up weaknesses in other places. For example, when I evaluate where I perform the best, it is often in how I display creativity. It is also where I risk grossly overinvesting my energy and find myself (when I am being honest with myself) covering up for areas where I underperform, including thinking strategically.

Understanding the personal, social, adaptable, and intentional elements, which taken together form the agile and relational systems, helps us understand how to cultivate belonging in real, tangible ways. As you work within your Agile and Relational systems, building out your leadership box, you will invariably expose blockages and misalignments—two of the most critical things to understand as it relates to having the capacity to invite people "inside your box" of belonging. When you understand the composition of your box, it is easier for you to understand where you are open and, more importantly, where you are closed off. The ability to leverage both the Agile and Relational systems helps you be more flexible and responsive to the people and concepts with which you are faced.

This framework amplifies the energy that cascades throughout leadership by alleviating any misconceptions, obstructions, or imbalances. Identifying misalignments between who we are internally and how we are experienced externally helps to dispel confusion and drive lasting performance. At Deutser, we encourage leaders to find a coach, someone who can guide them from behind or challenge them from the front, priming them to expand their self-awareness and address the sides of their box in different ways to further develop as leaders. We're not striving for perfection; we're striving for a deep and honest understanding of ourselves and how we lead with strength and agility in an increasingly disconnected world.

THE BOX AND OUR BIASES

One element that few like to address openly is the issue of bias. Breaking down biases is critical to belonging. Biases reflect our prejudices, whether in favor of or against something, some person, some group, or some experience. As with truth, power, and labeling, bias requires us to look at the dynamics involved. Understand, before we go further, that when we use the word "bias," we often think about the concept through a polarizing perspective—and immediately turn off. And, when we think of bias as a label, it is no wonder. But when we think about bias in its most simplistic form, we can begin to reflect more thoughtfully about those things in our minds and lives that may have contributed to it.

If we accept that we all have some form of bias and are willing to explore it with an open mind, we can learn and evolve. As part of this developmental work, it can be beneficial to consider how these biases show up in your day-to-day experiences and how they impact the ways in which you understand yourself (the personal side of the box), your interactions with others (the social side of the box), your responses to changes around you (the adaptable side of the box), and your ability to lead with purpose (the intentional side of the box). We can choose to look at each of the sides through various lenses as we challenge what we see and think. When we allow ourselves to challenge potential biases on each side of the box, it allows us to be more authentic, more open, and more willing to explore our leadership going forward. Leaders can examine their constructed box to help them recognize and reduce bias in themselves and others. Leading from this posture is vital. Begin to pay attention when you feel uncomfortable; dig deeper into that feeling. Where does it come from? What side of the leadership box might it be impacting or emanating from? Is there a bias that is coloring your perspective?

Unfortunately, when we begin to explore our biases, we often confront the tumultuous experience of shame. We cannot, as leaders, fully construct our box and reflect on our biases without acknowledging shame's role in holding us back from growth.

By turning us off from discourse, shame propels an avoidance that we struggle to accept. Shame directly impedes our ability to address our biases and lead within the box framework. Specifically, shame impacts our ability to be mindful by turning us off from enacting the deep, internal work necessary to address biases, foster fairness, and ultimately promote belonging in the organizations and communities we are part of. Shame makes us unwilling to approach new and evolving situations with perspective. Even saying the word out loud can be uncomfortable, especially when making eye contact with someone or while attempting to hold ourselves accountable.

Sometimes shame is personal, often for private reasons, but there is another form of shame rampant in the workplace today: the feeling of being ashamed. When discussing biases, we often know we're not personally responsible for the many factors that led to societal bias, yet many of us are ashamed that these factors have impeded progress at all, often from our membership in a particular demographic (e.g., being a white man, being over fifty, living in an urban area, being a Southerner, or having membership in a political party or social group). The line between personal shame and group shame has become blurred. We cannot build our leadership box, nor can we recognize and reduce the negative impact of biases in ourselves and others, without addressing shame directly.

None of us is immune to the impact of shame and biases that accompany it. And while becoming more aware, particularly when it comes to shame or fear, it is an important first step (one that will help us effectively construct our leadership boxes in ways that engender belonging), we can't stop here. We also must proactively embrace the agile system, expanding our minds from a place of humility as we get new information and remaining in the throes of change with grace. Leaders can embrace change and stay connected to others by soliciting consistent feedback from others about how biases may be clouding our judgment or impacting our behaviors. None of us are perfect, and we will all revert to biased patterns of thinking and behaving at times. However, we find that reflecting on various forms of bias, leveling up your awareness of where these biases come from, and recognizing how they may affect your interactions with others can begin to help you mitigate their power and prevalence in your leadership. Why? Because learning about what unconscious bias looks like and thinking through examples makes you more attuned and aware. Bias becomes more salient to you, so your brain can pick up on biased patterns more frequently. It will allow you to return to your Box of Belonging and be more open to invite others who are different from you deeper inside. It will also allow them to increase their understanding and trust of you as their leader.

SELF-AWARENESS AND BELONGING

Cultivating self-awareness is essential for leaders looking to clarify and define their box, as it prompts a thorough, honest, and continuous evaluation of oneself and others. As noted, we at Deutser think about our box model as three-dimensional—about the internal and the external aspects of the self, as well as the Agile and Relational systems. The dimensions show how I think about myself, how others think about me, how I lead through change, and how intentional and purposeful I am in my actions as a leader—all aspects of self-awareness. Building the box begins with the ability to see ourselves through an honest lens and extends much further to thinking about our relationships, intentionality, and agility. It's all connected, interwoven, and essential to creating the multifaceted experience of belonging for ourselves and others.

Leaders with high self-awareness are better able to accurately perceive themselves. They know the areas they struggle with and their strengths, as well as how their behaviors and emotions affect others. Self-aware leaders are authentic and have learned humility, having done the necessary yet often difficult self-reflection and mindfulness study to achieve this higher state of emotional intelligence. They are also better able to manage and regulate their emotions. They're less caught up in themselves, in the thoughts and passions that can sometimes hijack our brains and take us out of the present. Their ability to get out of their own heads and find presence enables them to approach contentious issues, hold challenging conversations, and endure periods of uncertainty from a place of empathy and with concern for others' welfare.

Self-aware leaders are better able to create experiences of belonging because they bring two types of peace: internal (self-reflective) and external (relationship oriented). According to psychologist and researcher Dr. Tasha Eurich, the internal component of self-awareness reflects one's ability to clearly appraise their own values, motivations, and dreams—how they fit with their environments (e.g., how they think and feel, or understand their strengths and weaknesses) and their impact on others. In turn, the external, relationship-oriented component reflects one's knowledge about how other people see them, considering the same factors included in the definition of internal self-awareness. Eurich's research shows that people who understand how others view them are more adept at demonstrating empathy and considering others' perspectives. Employees tend to demonstrate stronger and better relationships with leaders high in external self-awareness and view them as generally more effective. However, what Eurich has found in her work—and what I've echoed and extended here with the box framework—is that leaders are most effective and best able to foster belonging when they are high in both internal and external self-awareness, versus cultivating one at the expense of the other. These leaders strive to understand themselves clearly, doing the internal work of mindfulness and effective introspection, and seek out honest feedback from others regarding their behavioral and emotional impact. They understand that self-awareness is about navigating the delicate balance between these perspectives.

We want and expect leaders to be self-aware and to be introspective about their leadership teams and their tendencies. Being able to ask the right questions and get to the root of connection is challenging, even for the best leaders. Often, we begin a workshop with an exercise called "why." The point is to provoke raw, unfiltered questions and to teach leaders about the damage that asking "why" can cause. This exercise is the only time we advocate for using the word. Leaders think that asking "why" questions will help us get the truth, but because we lack awareness of many aspects of our unconscious, asking "why" questions tends to entrench existing beliefs and sustain our biased patterns of thinking. Instead, we teach leaders to focus on "what" and "how" questions, operating like a coach and leading from an objective, future-focused, and empowered place rather than a reactive place of subjectivity and bias. Asking "what" and "how" instead of "why" tends to create dialogue rather than shut down the conversation before it begins. As a result, those on the other side of these discussions will be less likely to feel accused of something—another essential element of creating connectedness, security, and group affinity, one that allows even the most challenging conversations to occur as individuals share their honest perspectives.

THE BOX AND BELONGING-FOCUSED LEADERSHIP

As the box of belonging evolves and changes with us, it becomes an important leadership tool. The bottom part of the box, which hosts elements of our identity, will rarely change, but the top and the swirl of the environment around it will always be changing—not just influencing, but also challenging each of its sides. This fluidity is to be expected and embraced. Likewise, our relationships are in a constant, necessary, and healthy tension with and within the sides of the box, as well as with and within the Relational and Agility systems. It is important to know your box—to work on it, reflect on it, and challenge it by working to overcome your biases.

Belonging-focused leaders see how the elements of the box connect and test themselves regularly. They care about enhancing their ability to relate to people from all backgrounds, and they know that this all begins with understanding the self through multiple lenses. You're not striving for perfection; you're striving for a deep and honest understanding of yourself and how you lead through relationships in an evolving yet increasingly disconnected world.

The world will challenge you, and so will all the people around you looking to you for leadership. They will lift you up only when it is convenient, and work to tear you down to serve their best self-interest. Your box can counter them by reinforcing your strengths and uniqueness while providing a framework to shield you against external shots and internal doubts. Most importantly, you will know where you belong, as a prerequisite for creating the space and capacity for others to belong. Giving structure to concept provides a powerful construct where belonging can flourish and deep connections reliably occur.

Chapter 8

THE NEW TBD—TO BE DESIGNED

NEXT AND NEXT AFTER THAT

'm not sure how we got into the habit of pausing by proclaiming something *to be determined*, but I can tell you that right out of the gate, it's a mistake. The Belonging Rules demand a different understanding and an intentional approach to change. Untangling from our tendency to operate from a defensive posture requires significant time and effort. This leaves us to react impulsively, even thoughtlessly, at times as we underestimate how quickly and fiercely change will come. We must own the onus of designing our future and reject thinking or believing it will just come together. We cannot wait and allow change to happen to us or for us; rather, that need for action of which we have discussed throughout this book is a hallmark of the intentionality required of today's leaders.

As leaders, we must insert ourselves into the heart of conversations, debates, and decisions—regardless of how difficult and unpleasant they seem. Thus, TBD, from this point forward in your leadership lexicon, must be understood as *To Be Designed*. It is within this holistic construct that all five of the rules take shape, are nurtured, and become fully viable.

We cannot turn into the power without understanding the structures in our way and the intentional design required to expertly go through them. We cannot listen without labels without a designed approach to listening, one where we approach conversations and conflicts with the intent to learn from and understand people as human beings. We cannot choose identity over purpose without a thoughtfully understood, articulated, and designed identity, a clearly delineated cultural ecosystem that describes the whole of your organization or your being. We cannot challenge everything without a design element of how we are going to approach the challenge from a position of strength and a desire to create something more profound. We cannot demand 100% of the truth without a designed threshold that opens a pathway capable of closing the gap between 80% and 100%. Design is at the heart of how we access the wonders of what the rules require to bring each one to life.

To Be Designed immediately conveys commitment and deliberate action rather than passivity. The very act of designing acknowledges that you're going to update, curate, reconfigure, and mold something that doesn't yet exist. It announces that ingenuity is going to be part of the expectation rather than a surprise reaction to forces that develop with little input from you or even without you. And, as we design, we're creating capacity for the sum of what our belonging together produces. We're not looking to control the narrative, as is popular to say. We are talking about willful design that invites, equips, and relies on interplay to create increasingly positive momentum toward the shared desired outcome. This act of making a space where our best is called upon and can engage creates the capacity for all to make meaningful impact. Imagine a space within which everyone collectively performs their best work, is unified in shared vision, and recognizes their fit because of who they are as individuals. This is the type of design that belonging relies on and inspires.

A DESIRED FUTURE STATE

Your future should never be left to chance. The future is yours to own, to control, or, more appropriately said, to direct in whatever way you can. The future is yours to be excited and energized by. The future is within your grasp. But it must be designed by you and grounded in your own identity.

Design creates the bridge between your current state and a desired future state. Undoubtedly, the future will happen. The question is—is it a future that happens to you or one that you have thoughtfully contemplated, curated, and constructed? Fate is not an answer; action and ownership is. Thus, the importance of TBD—as in, to be designed by you.

It is the very reason I approach every situation with a TBD mindset. Think about the energy shift that occurs when the "D" is changed from "determined" to "designed." Imagine multiple options. Give yourself space to design; allow yourself the gift of choice between not only potential pathways but also the minute details that provide richness and nuance, infused to change the trajectory of any solution set we choose to adopt and a reality you create.

How you address the future is dependent on how you approach the problem and imagine yourself as part of the solution. I see myself as a designer. I design dreams. I design solutions. I design futures. I design connections. I design metaphorical bridges and spaces, real and perceived, to bring people together. Design is fundamental to how I see the future and the possibilities that belong to me and to those around me. Too often, leaders leave design to the "creative people" or the strategists to develop. But why? I often hear responses that boil down to "I am not creative." As humans, we each have the capacity to be creative—in our individual and unique ways. It may not be artistic, but we can each be distinctive in our thoughts, plans, words, and actions. Design gifts each of us with differentiation. We must allow ourselves the authority and responsibility to be in control of our unique pathway forward. While the world pushes for conformity, design expresses our individuality.

LEADING WITH DESIGN

Intentional design requires the innate understanding of leadership alchemy—the willingness to take in diverse elements without knowing how they will mix with what you already know and have experienced. This is vital to modern leadership—the openness we've coaxed throughout this book will bring to light previously disconnected concepts, ideas, people, and things in a manner that fosters all to ultimately connect, redefine, rise, and propel forward toward newfound and amazing outcomes. This alchemy relies on commitment from all to the Belonging Rules, which must not be left on the periphery of leadership but rightfully centered at the core of leadership. Belonging leadership must be embraced not simply for what it is, but for the potential it promises. This style of leadership facilitates the future through unapologetic inclusivity and openness. When we are open to others, we find ways to become more open and accepting of ourselves.

Designers ponder aspirational outcomes, and through a process of skilled trial and occasional error, they build something magical. Designing the experience of belonging is not a one-time effort but an ongoing process that requires thoughtfulness, attention, and refinement—like all great design. As the workplace and the broader cultural landscape continue evolving, organizations and leaders must also adapt their practices and policies to ensure that each person feels valued and included. This might involve regularly soliciting feedback from employees, conducting belonging assessments, piloting appropriate interventions with employees, and adjusting workplace policies and practices based on honest conversations and a culture that encourages regular feedback. The efforts that actualize belonging require work and intermittent recalibration.

Ultimately, designing the experience of belonging is about creating and sustaining a workplace culture that prioritizes the five rules. Embedding the five rules intentionally throughout the organization can foster a more engaged, positive, productive, and satisfied workforce. As we know from our research and the work of leading scientists in this field, designing the experience of belonging is not only good for employees but also good for the organization, resulting in improved outcomes, increased innovation, and a more vibrant reputation in the broader community. It not only *feels* right; it also *is* right for you and others.

Design is an expression of identity for all of us. It embodies and emboldens who you are and shares that belongingness with the world so that others who are like-minded can find you and those who are seeking what you offer can be recruited and joyfully join. And, while the like-minded may in fact be actively searching for you, there are those who at a cursory glance don't recognize you or identify with you—the same is true for you with them. But, when you are open to a different design, one that is centered on belonging, you can begin to break down the structures, biases, and blockages to broaden your perspectives and actively seek what is different from you. This intentionality is palpable yet doesn't feel forced. There is an elegance and courageousness that buoy this approach.

In so many ways, this is what modern leadership is missing and requires. It calls for a boldness and originality that may force many leaders outside their comfort zone. It also recognizes the vulnerability in leaders to not just plan but also actively and aggressively challenge the potential futures that are ahead. After all, whatever future is ahead is yours to design.

DESIGNING AT DEUTSER

While much focus in this chapter has been given to metaphoric space and mindset, at Deutser, we are always thoughtful about the physical spaces in which the future is to incubate, be born, and continue to grow. Too often, the biggest decisions leaders make are made in their overly corporate boardrooms or closed-in offices. Ask yourself how that encourages creativity or positivity. Most often, it encourages expected, corporate design that reinforces a style of interactions left over from decades of manipulated power structures. Much of the time, that physical construct makes it harder to move forward in creating new dynamics because the physical space discourages it or even physically does not allow for it. Yes, space has that power. It is why the mind space is crucial and the physical space fundamental to design. It does not require a fun, wacky, overly creative space—although science shows that can be helpful. It does require intentionality of environments that can best propel your originality. Even a home office environment requires thoughtfulness and possible change to generate a space more conducive to your needed design solutions.

Our deep dedication to design motivates us to understand the brain and how it functions. After all, the brain is the design center for our lives, work, and contributions. We understand that where you create—both the physical and mental space—can be as important as any factor to determining the final output. We have built highly unique physical spaces for leaders and teams in businesses, for collegiate and professional sports teams, and for leaders and organizations interested in designing the experience of belonging—we think of our own spaces, our offices and Learning Labs, to be like Willy Wonka's factory for people wanting to be there to explore and expand their potential.

Leadership games on the ceiling and floor, clouds on the ground with floating game boards, exercises on every wall, lights flashing, creative interruptions, and intentional distractions. This is core to Dimensional Leadership Learning. Our unique approach embraces the traditional learning modalities—auditory, visual, tactile, and kinesthetic—and incorporates originality, intentional disruptions, and unexpected creative interactions. All these are designed to induce positive stimuli to neutralize and overcome the negativity or reality-based thinking that leaders bring to every conversation. When you take into consideration that humans have eighty thousand thoughts a day with 90% repeated and 85% of those negative, we then understand the desperate need for something to jolt our creative responses. Our Leadership Learning Labs and Dimensional Leadership Learning become a powerful antidote for the traditional and more expected functional spaces leaders so often use to discuss the most complex issues.

Often the gravity of those traditional rooms makes problem-solving feel like a rinse-and-repeat cycle. We apply research on adult learning, team building, and leadership development programs in original and inspiring ways. We encourage active participation through storytelling and role-playing along with interactive group and individual exercises. We reinforce learning as a process and not a single event. We use one-on-one coaching to help learners identify their unique areas of growth and provide materials that support their individual learning pathways. We know that inputs are just as important as outputs—so we take care to design programs that are tailored to each client and individual leader. We evaluate the success of our programs using quantitative and qualitative data. We are never designing simple solutions—we just try to make them appear that way. And we always infuse creativity because it is what opens the mind to possibility. It is fundamental to belonging leadership—never complicating, always simplifying, and always inviting a multitude of diverse thoughts and perspectives to fill the spaces of our rooms and thought processes.

We will design anything. And everything has an original perspective, even if works to bring elements of the past forward. We design to make people, things, businesses whole. We find the gaps and fill them. We think of every solution through a design lens. We infuse color—even when it is black and white—through energy, words, and emotion. We understand that design is core to the necessary human connection that leads to spaces and, ultimately, openness for belonging.

INFUSING FUN INTO CHANGE

It is always interesting to me when leaders are initially reticent about bringing their teams to our playland for leadership. They often question how fun has any role in bridging the most complex issues. It does. And it provides important exploration and connection, as we can experience others in a different way. This brings out aspects that we've overlooked or have previously been unknown to us that create futures that have yet to be designed.

One of my great inspirations and earliest lessons in the importance of fun in building inclusive communities is summer camp. To most people, it is a fun experience for young kids. To me and many of the people I went to camp with over fifteen summers, it was an everyday lesson in leadership, community building, and belonging. It taught me every lesson imaginable about being a leader, a parent, and a designer of the future—mine and others.

My experiences at summer camp set me up for a life of success—even when I wasn't successful. From my first day, I was an outsider in every way. I was one of four boys from Texas at the over-five-hundred-person camp in western Massachusetts; I was not an athlete at this intense, boys-only sports camp—then and today one of the oldest private boys' camps in the country. Camp Greylock, as it is commonly referred to, has produced generations of leaders, all of whom started there as young boys.

What stood out at Greylock was the unique identity of the camp carefully crafted and fiercely protected by the two camp owners, Bert Margolis and Irv Schwartz. They were the perfect yin and yang to each other. Bert was a soulful Renaissance man. A philosopher by nature, he loved the outdoors and enjoyed sharing its wonders. My fellow campers and I had early access to a man who lived with his whole being and saw all activity, even down to how we dealt with problems, as life. Irv was a fierce competitor by nature and in practice. He taught us how to show up for each other and for any sport, play hard, employ strategy, and win. He also taught us how to lose—with a generous spirit and by reflecting on that loss. We were given a framework to understand that we were expected back on the playing field with enthusiasm and renewed commitment to win again. They were intentional in how they designed every experience and every opportunity to build meaningful, lasting relationships and create space to grow young men of character.

It was a place where, over the fifteen years that I was there (four as a camper and eleven as a counselor and leader), I greatly felt I belonged, where I enjoyed the people and the involvement, and where I always felt safe to be myself. In fact, it was the only place I felt totally free to be me. For eight weeks of every summer, we were under the tutelage and direction of these two leaders, assisted by a host of counselors and coaches. In addition, we forged deep friendships, and although campers and counselors came from all over the world to Camp Greylock, many of us stayed in touch and even got together during other times of the year. In fact, many of us are still deeply and emotionally connected forty-plus years later.

All relationships at Greylock were built on trust (reinforced by radical accountability) and deep human connection (facilitated by constant shared activities). No one wanted to let Bert or Irv down, nor did we in any way want to disappoint their clearly stated (over and over again) expectations. Their mission was to build good citizens, Renaissance men, leaders who would live up to certain standards and contribute in positive ways to the communities where they lived. We were told:

"Be the bigger person."

"Never be a bully, and don't tolerate bullying of anyone."

"Do it because it is the right thing to do."

"Always be respectful of women."

"Never slide with your feet up—never, ever hurt anyone in your own actions."

"If the ball appears to be out but you are unsure, call it in."

"Win the right way."

"It's okay to show affection—even for people of your own gender."

And almost all of us carried these principles forward in our professional careers, setting a foundation of success, accountability, and connection. The mastery of Bert and Irv was the intricate design of the expectations they set for us. The value system they challenged us with set an impeccably high standard with boundaries that were different from those of any other camp. Nothing that they did was accidental. In fact, it was as elegantly designed as any leadership teaching anywhere.

Greylock remains with me every day of my life. It was the first place, outside my family, where I knew I belonged. But, more than that, it taught me that we design our future from the very beginning. Design starts early and is always available to you.

REDESIGNING AN INDUSTRY

Jason Siegel has had a steady, amazing leadership trajectory that began with the teachings of Camp Greylock and has extended to his role as the bold leader of an innovative, culture-focused, multi-strategy hedge fund, BHS Solutions. He has turned the financial industry upside down by prioritizing the heart and soul of the human spirit—and many of his lessons of fair play he learned from Bert Margolis. He has created a space where the culture is to be designed with each interaction by the people who live in it every day. Jason embodies belonging leadership. He saw an opportunity to create a space of inclusivity in an industry that has long been closed off. He saw an opportunity to challenge the most fundamental beliefs in the business and focus on what he believed was right and best for people.

Jason brought a compelling vision to design and transformed both the business industry and the hedge fund industry. He rejected the belief that hedge fund people only care about money and tolerate working with anyone, anywhere, to get the highest returns. He convinced the company's leadership that he could create a new operational model with a primary emphasis on culture where he would recruit, retain, and incentivize the highest-caliber talent—understanding that he would be bringing in top producers while initially promising them far less capital to manage. Brookfield signed off on the model he developed, while perhaps not fully understanding how far their new leader would go to emphasize culture or its importance to performance.

That culture—intentionally created from the onset—developed the company DNA in the form of a cultural ecosystem. The second week in his new position, Jason arranged for his starting employees to spend a week at the Deutser Clarity Institute. He began to build the business from scratch, starting with the cultural foundation. Every painstaking detail was discussed, including a 9.5-hour debate on the meaning of "integrity," which ultimately became "integrity lived," one of their budding humanized values. It was in this debate around that singular value that the BHS DNA was formulated and cultivated as additional values were added. It became clear to all participating that the values—intentionality focused, mindfulness practiced, integrity lived, grit forged, and ingenuity imagined—were sacrosanct. Jason agonized over every element of his cultural foundation. He did this because he knew every image, word, and proclamation was vital to attract the people he wanted to join but also to unite them in accountability. He was unwilling to have any of the words or behaviors defined "as the business got going" and instead insisted on being intentional and mindful (two of his personal favorite values) from the inception through execution to sustainable effort that would sync with every intentional detail.

This leader claimed identity as the centerpiece of belonging for the top talent in the field.

This vision also was captured when the name of the firm was created—Brookfield Hedge Solutions—with the "H" in "Hedge" silent. That H̲, with an underline to represent an element in the periodic table, is embraced as the human element in their work and culture. It is also their hedge (read with the silent "H" as "edge"). It reinforces their promise to build a company with people as the greatest differentiator to attract, retain, protect, and invest in.

The hiring process my team designed for them included extensive leadership and mental assessments along with behavioral interviews where candidates would know the firm's leadership and leadership would know the candidates. All could equally recognize the fit designed to produce the desired results. And their physical space was equally crafted to communicate their intentions. The design of office spaces is modeled after the most welcoming and luxury spa-like hotels in the world, complete with a library (for book clubs) and an Institute for Leadership Development. A visiting team of JP Morgan's top executives shared: "We have never seen, much less dreamed, anything like this . . . there is a seriousness about the development here that is palpable." It goes back to the values—every element is designed off that platform.

The firm constructed a differentiated business that has provided successful returns to the parent company, not costing them one cent since their inception as they built the business from one employee to now over seventy-five, four years later and through a pandemic. They have attracted some of the biggest and most respected hedge-fund managers and analysts in the business—many who left positions managing over $1 billion to starting at BHS by managing less than $300 million. These managers and analysts wanted something different and believed that they could help design the future here. The company has not just talked about culture and being different; it has invested in its own Clarity Institute for ongoing leadership learning in their New York office, including weekly meditation, yoga sessions, leadership development sessions, one-on-one leadership coaching, and book clubs (with more than 90% office participation). They have done the impossible by maintaining an elite workforce with retention of more than 95% over a four-year period. They are living the intention that even the most competitive, stress-filled industry can be better and more profitable when intentionally designed to invite and care for people. When you surround yourself with what brings out your best, your body of work begins to reflect your progression. Great leaders are always transitioning and designing for the future. Leaders own their success wherever they go and whatever they do next.

MERGERS BY DESIGN

The BHS model is one we carry over into the mergers-and-acquisitions space. The lessons of caring for people, placing a financial value on culture, and understanding the human element in complex business deals is part of an intentional design we demand in these situations. In this space, we take two distinct identities and must find a way to design one more impactful organization. Mashing them together never works long term. Nor does it yield the financial reward expected at the onset of the merger. Neither can continue as they were, and all deserve to belong in one cohesive whole. It is why their shared future must be designed. The pieces that are supposed to come together don't always fit—but with intentional work and collaborative design, the sum of the parts can add up to a brilliant new whole.

In a recent merger where we helped to facilitate the cultural integration, I was struck by the unspoken parts—the perceptions of one company by its geographical idiosyncrasies and the other by its perceived rigid culture. Two global companies with headquarters on two different sides of the globe. We worked with them first on culture—people, systems, safety—core areas that are so often saved for the end, while finance and operations are typically prioritized. But we always start with people. When you begin with people, remaining cultural adjustments and enhancements can occur in a more holistic way.

In this particular merger, we combined leadership teams—half from one company and half from the other. They were brought together for a workshop. Three days of detailed discussion to carve out a newly imagined and desired shared future gave them a vision of how they could come together to achieve extraordinary success. They equally participated to begin to dream—yes, dreaming is a core element of our work, and our floors are painted with blue skies and wispy clouds for leaders to walk around—about this future through a lens of positivity, empowerment, and fun. We created exercises using custom card decks with personal questions to build trust among team members first meeting and building connection. We used blank ceramic tiles for them to draw their picture of the future to be built on accountability, and we put a giant cup full of LEGOs on the table for small groups to collaboratively and creatively build their vision for the company and its culture. Some of the pieces were LEGO branded, and some were generic—in other words, they were like so many of our companies: a lot of pieces may not be designed to fit together. Still, the challenge remains—it is our job to design a picture where they do fit and belong. Broken up into ten teams of six (three Danish and three American), they were given fifteen minutes to create the picture of the company's future—they had to use every piece, regardless of if it fit, and they had to tell a story with their creation and in their own words. Their creativity blew everyone away.

Each team created a different image—and a different story, connected by the emerging shared identity of the company. The emphasis was different in each one. Ideas and priorities came to light. They physically leaned in, they talked, they challenged, they laughed, they added their unique touch, and four of the groups even put their stories to music. They reminded us of something important with the LEGO exercise. Sometimes you can design more with a laugh than with anything else. The instinct for some to add music added panache and infused an emotional feel to what they were proposing. The group learned a lot about each other that day. They also took a step toward their shared new future by seeing what they could become rather than holding on to what each had been. They also used all the pieces they were given and found ways to make all the pieces fit—even if they were not supposed to fit. That may have been the most impactful lesson as they thought about people and finding ways to make all fit in the new organization.

SOMETIMES THE WORK FINDS YOU

Mergers represent two companies coming together—often forcing employees to leave things behind in their companies. The sacrifice is real and, to some, too challenging to overcome. But, in sports, the sacrifice is core to being on a team. In fact, I love the locker room as a symbol of hope for our country and world. It represents so many of the inherent challenges of companies and individuals as well as society. People come from different backgrounds, with unique perspectives and experiences, yet all share the collective goals of winning, becoming champions, and defying the odds in some powerful way on an individual and team level.

Locker rooms, healthy ones at least, have a way of eliminating differences, accepting people for who they are, and not caring where people came from. They are where teammates come together to prepare for what is about to happen and where they return for a needed pep talk or to celebrate or bemoan the day's events. It is a space where everyone has a role and must bring their best around a common purpose. The best locker rooms share a deep identity. Locker rooms are about trust and expectations—for the individual and each of the teammates and coaches.

But, more, locker rooms are often a melting pot: socioeconomics, race, politics, religion—they are home to everything. Locker rooms are unique in that they are redefined with each new team each year. The same players need to quickly adapt and can have fundamentally different locker rooms from year to year. They are forced to talk and share—they cannot hide—literally anything. It is all exposed. They don't have a choice; their belonging space is quite small—the actual physical size that it is.

When they leave that safe space, the eyes of the community and the fans (short for fanatics) are now on them and what they are about to design on their field or court. These fanatics feel a connection, sometimes a very deep one, and want the players to represent them—even when they don't know each other. They look at the team as a collective, and the players look at the fans the same way. It is an interdependent ecosystem. When one breaks the social contract, all are blamed. As a team, they must get to know one another, find something to like about each other, and trust each other. This is a business fundamental—people want to work and perform with people they know, like, and trust. When we take the locker room lessons out of the locker room, we have an ability to see through the societal issues that can rush in on us and just be humans, people who want to achieve something together.

When teams allow the outside into the locker room, they bring in influences that can either create deeper bonds or divisions. The best teams attack and swarm the issue to not let it fester. Others either don't recognize its power or hope it will go away with future wins. That rarely works, and the wins are not consistent. The coaches understand the necessary alchemy that is required and design experiences to promote belonging leadership so that every team member is not only invited in but also genuinely valued.

IT TAKES THE GUTS OF A LEADER

At times, societal issues and miscommunication divide teams. It can wreck a team when they allow differences to divide them or define them, and it shows in their performance. I've seen teams that held on to their differences to a point that it excluded the people next to them.

I have been in those locker rooms. In one situation, I was amazed when I discovered that the coach had abandoned the current team—he was busy coaching and scheming for the following weeks. He appeared more worried about the next class he was recruiting than the kids who'd already pledged their allegiance to him and were out there playing with heart and soul. The adult failed the kids, but the kids paid the price. Friendships unraveled, frustration was the norm, and this prominent team was losing in an embarrassing and public fashion. The attacks from the outside were relentless on social media and in the stands. Each day, the hurt grew and so did the divide. One-on-one meetings with several leaders exposed that there was no conversation among the players about their differing perspectives. Silos had developed, and players were in feedback loops with only those who shared their same perspectives. The team had become pitted against each other.

When I asked one of the leaders of the warring sides, "Have you and the other team leader talked?" He said, "Yeah, we're good." I said, "That is not what I asked. I asked, have you really talked? Has your coach helped to bridge a conversation and help you both listen to each other so you can design a path forward?" He again said, "We are good, and we are buds." I pushed one more time, harder, more forcefully: "Have you talked about race—how one of you is white and one is mixed race?" He said, "Oh. I guess not. Maybe we should." The next day, I met them as a leadership team—eighteen athletes with emerging leadership skills and no coaches. No introduction was given to them about me or why I was there—I was thrown in to heal the deep divide. I started by talking about how they saw the future, not the past. I talked about them having the chance to write their own story, design their own future. But the most vocal leaders were troubled and stuck. They didn't want to see a future—they wanted to be heard, and they wanted to stay stuck in the moment. The conversation disintegrated into yelling, first at the other race, then amongst each other—and anyone who had a moderate view was attacked. It wasn't until the player I had spoken with the previous day turned to his nemesis (at the time) and asked if he would stand by him and lead together that things began to shift. The player asked him not to change his mind, but to be open to another point of view. He asked his teammate to perform with him on the field. He then did that with each leader in the room. They stood in unity—one by one—and agreed to stand with each other, not apart from each other. The result was a series of wins, a winning record and a bowl victory that they designed. They became recognized for the divide they worked to heal off the field as well as their performance on it. Still, even with their successes, the leader was exposed for what he didn't do: design a locker-room culture where they all could belong.

Leaders who believe in belonging must be okay living and working in discomfort—even if it has the chance to backfire on them. The coach was unwilling to take risks, do what was difficult, be authentic, or create spaces for difficult conversations, and he ultimately lost his team. But the team found leaders that were willing to be vulnerable, to be exposed, and who were willing to work toward a future they not only designed but believed was possible. They designed it on their own. It is a powerful reminder that everything in our lives is for us to design—even when our coaches, teammates, boards, bosses, and families have other thoughts. If the players had allowed that season to be determined, they wouldn't have won another game, and their story would have been part of the bad lore of the university for years to come. Instead, their story, while not of a national championship, is an indelible reminder of the power we all have to design our own tomorrow.

THE WHOLENESS OF BELONGING

We believe passionately that belonging is based on making and being whole, even though it may require you to put broken pieces together in a new way. This is true for the locker room, the schoolroom, and the boardroom. Our world feels broken too often. We are faced with daily challenges that create chasms in our belief systems and hope for a more inclusive world. Yet we still wake up each day with the belief that things can once again be whole. It is far too easy to look at the breaks in our society and feel helpless. Instead, we must challenge ourselves to be part of an intentional relook at what is and what can and must be for ourselves and the next generations. We must stop looking at the broken pieces, the perceived societal cracks, and the gaps in connections and start to highlight what we actually share. When we design a picture of the future and it is built on what we have in common, then we have a platform to begin the necessary and deeply desired change that lies ahead of us.

An exercise that we have adopted and designed to address this broken feeling is what we call the "art of the whole"— it is also known as *kintsugi* or the art of the broken. With our view of positivity, we intentionally think about things in a desired whole state, even as they exist in a broken world or environment. When I think about designing spaces for belonging, I think about all the disparate parts and pieces coming together, creating the wholeness and connectivity we crave as humans. Yet, our lives are in pieces—separated by various situations or work, life, and personal challenges. So, we bring people together and ask them to physically break things. This gives everyone a chance to mirror what has already happened in our lives. It also levels us to the same grounding with which to start—here we are, emotions and all, with our colleagues and friends. We bring teams together, give them a beautiful bowl, hand them a burlap sack and hammer, and ask them to hit and shatter the bowl. Most people make the first hit with medium force, not knowing what to expect—often not breaking the bowl but feeling the vibration and piercing sound of the collision. Then they realize it is going to take a harder hit, and the sounds of shattering bowls fill the room. The pieces are then spilled out on the table. It is a mess. Some are sad and think, "What a waste of a beautiful bowl." Others wonder, "What are we going to do with this?" Next comes the task of putting the pieces back together. A metaphor for life. A metaphor for anything broken, anything destroyed. And, like in life, the pieces don't fit back neatly. Once the bowl is glued back together in whatever form the pieces dictate, the imperfections are highlighted with gold paint. This creates a beauty in the bowl's brokenness and becomes something new. What we do with this exercise is demonstrate how extraordinary our broken world and lives really are; how we can highlight and embrace imperfection instead of hiding it; how we can break and put things back together. Coming apart and bringing together in an enlightened way is a daily function of leaders and people. Because we believe so strongly that each of us has a leader already within us, take note that leadership can emerge from any vantage point. That one new perspective can bring all together. Yet, instead of relishing the rebuild and appreciating the challenge in the midst of brokenness, we too often and too easily throw things away and start over. This is a reminder that imperfection is fundamental to and embraced by great design.

Belonging leadership sometimes requires us to make hard decisions and break things up, even in a high-functioning business or team environment, so that we can put them together in a more intentional way. This is true for coaches navigating the changing landscape of both professional sports as well as collegiate sports. Teams are broken up every year, and a more beautiful, higher-performing version is expected to be constructed. So, too, is the case for organizations, individuals, and families. The belonging leader accepts the responsibility to both create the necessary fractures and to build back an organization or team that embraces the whole of its people.

THE DESIGN IS OURS

The future is indeed for us to design. When I think about the tens of thousands of people we interact with each year through our work, I become inspired with what can be for our evolving world through their hopefulness and desire to do and be more. It is obvious where leaders get stuck and where they get motivated to affect lasting change. People

In this final exercise, you will design your own version of belonging. What does it mean to belong in your organization? What's your desired future state and how will you get there, igniting and sustaining a culture of belonging along the way?

Design your belonging story, build it however you want, and using the questions as prompts, figure out what it will take to achieve this meaningful, connected, empowered experience.

BELONGING TO BE DESIGNED

Why do I feel like I belong?

Why do I care about belonging?

Why does each rule matter in designing belonging?

What is 100% of the truth, and how will my organization get there?

How will I listen without labels?

How will I encourage others to do the same?

TBD

What is my current versus desired future state for each of the five rules?

What gaps do I need to close?

What does the future of belonging mean to me?

What is the first step I can take toward building that future?

How will I know if I've achieved success?

What can I do to create identity over purpose?

Where will I turn into the power?

What power structures can I lean into, and which ones do I need to dismantle?

How do I understand the collective identity of my organization?

want change—they just want it within the defined organizational identity and social contract that they signed up for. It is up to us as leaders to deliver on that promise.

The future has no plans. We are the ones with the plans—and the vision, the dreams, and the wherewithal to create the future. We cannot allow it to happen to us or allow it to be determined for us. We must be actively part of its creation. That is the spirit of what the Belonging Rules are all about. Changing the future, one decision, one act, one person at a time. We can each commit daily to finding our own spaces to turn into the power, to listen without labels, to choose identity over purpose, to challenge everything, and to demand 100% of the truth. It's your journey. It's your potential. It is your life, and it's your decision how it extends beyond you. It's your decision to invite people into your world and to be invited into someone else's world. The rules give the power back to you to be the transformational leader, the belonging leader, of your own life and business. How will you think about belonging?

To me, belonging is where we hold space for something of shared importance. It is where we come together on values, purpose, and identity; a space of acceptance where agreement is not required but a shared framework is understood; where there is an invitation into the space; an intentional choice to take part in; something vital to a sense of connection, security, and acceptance.

Belonging is a way of life and the only way to lead. When you believe in belonging and believe your future is TBD, you begin to create the world you want to live in and lead in. You challenge your own ideas and biases and are open to wildly different possibilities. You create a space for others and yourself, and that is where the alchemy and the magic collide to change tomorrow.

You have the tools. All it takes is conviction and courage—and if you are a leader in these times, you already have it. Allow the Belonging Rules to become your way of leadership and life. After all, it's all to be designed. By you.

ACKNOWLEDGMENTS

Admittedly, I was not sure I wanted to tackle a topic as potentially controversial as this one. But I believe with all my heart that it is a conversation that must be had at so many different levels across our society, our businesses, our universities, and even our families. And it was all the people around me who encouraged, supported, demanded, and deeply believed it was and is not only an important topic, but the right time for it.

Through this process, I was inspired by so many people who wanted to share, in the most vulnerable ways, their stories and understandings of belonging. They didn't just share their wins—they shared their struggles and setbacks. I am reminded and inspired by my client and mentor who shared, "We don't have to agree to belong." That is the spirit of this book.

There are things that I have shared that I deeply believe in. There are things in this book that I explored openly—simply to provoke thought and begin the necessary conversations required to invite people in and to genuinely connect on a human level. There are things in the book you will agree with and some you will disagree with and even become frustrated by. That is the purpose of the words—to think, to challenge, and hopefully to affect whatever change is important to you.

I would not have had the courage or strength to share my thoughts so openly if it weren't for the people whom I love, respect, and am honored to live and work with each and every day. It is because of you that I belong. And, in each page, I hope you see where your words, heart, and wisdom are shared so that the important conversation of belonging can begin.

Jill, Ashley, and Andrew, you are my heart and soul. I love you each more than you will ever know. Jill, thank you for believing, even when it takes us to places we never imagined. You believe in me more than anyone, and it fuels my soul and powers my dreams. You are my everything. Ashley and Andrew, there are no words for the love I have for you. You believe in me and us with so much passion and love. I am inspired by you and in awe of you both. You have accomplished and continue to accomplish at levels that are unimaginable to me. Your brilliance, your creativity, your drive, your kindness, your understanding of what is right and true, and your love and your passion for life inspires me and lifts me up every minute of every day. Your hearts and souls are so pure, beautiful, and wonderful. Jill, Ashley, and Andrew, you are each the inspiration for this book.

Mom and Dad, you believed in me before anyone. And I don't know of a day in my life that that belief ever wavered. No matter what I did, you cheered me forward. You showed me what lasting love is and how to smile on the rainiest of days. You challenged me. You taught me everything I know to be a father, son, friend, employee, leader, and most of all citizen who gives to others. Most of all, you loved me and made sure I belonged, even when I didn't. Debbie and Steven, and Sarah and Hance, you showed me what it means to be family, to love unconditionally, to work as family and to love as family. You are such tremendous blessings in my life, and I am grateful every day to call you MY brother and sister. Sarah, I love our friendship and all we share. My grandparents and Jill's grandparents showed what it means to overcome, to persevere, to create community, and to infuse the most important concept throughout every element of family—enduring love. Your stories inspired me and let me know that as immigrants, entrepreneurs, and community leaders you can achieve anything your mind can dream. Frann and Jeff, I am so grateful for your love, your strength, and continued belief in me. Your support is noticed and appreciated every day. Harris and Martha, the love you exude and kindness you share is inspiring. And, to my family everywhere, you inspire me!

Nancy H., you have an unbelievable way with words and making the most complex concepts understandable. But, most of all, you are one of my most important and trusted thought partners and a true friend. No one will ever understand the countless hours of thinking, talking, debating, and writing together. You have the most magical way of stringing words to create pure magic. I am grateful for you every day. Greg R., thank you for the inspiration you give to me. You see things that no one else can begin to see. I am grateful for your vision, your brilliance, and your partnership. Thank you for pushing me to bring belonging to life—without your challenge, there would be no belonging rules. Matt H., you didn't have to believe. But you did. You went all in with me on this book. Others were afraid to take on a potentially controversial topic. You were strong, bold, and visionary. You saw what others were unwilling to see. I am so excited to publish this book with you and so many more. Yes, you delighted me every step of the way. Shawn Achor, I will never forget your words years ago encouraging me to write and tell my story. Thank you for the positivity you bring not only to me, but to the world. You make me happy. David Eagleman, thank you for your partnership and for saving lives with us. My brain grows in such interesting ways every time we talk.

Belonging Rules is truly the outgrowth of a team like no other. I have never had people in my life like each of my Deutser family, who are willing to go all in and absolutely love what you do—and it shows. The words in this book are from your hearts and minds. Izzy, wow. What a difference you have made and continue to make in my work and life every day. I hope you beam with pride seeing your research, thinking, words, and unbelievable judgement on every page. Thank you for your partnership on this book and our Institute for Belonging. Ashley, you were the first interview and the one person whom I trust more than anyone to give me honest feedback and brilliant counsel. You elevate every thought, challenge content, and fiercely protect our ideas and each of us. Truly amazing. Alan, thank you for your leadership and brilliance in all you do. Thanks for inspiring me and challenging me! Diane, words cannot express my gratitude for your creative genius and amazing heart. Your work and thinking are infused throughout this book. Grateful beyond words. Christy, over all these years, you continue to amaze me with your creative brilliance. Thank you for bringing all the thinking to life through brilliant design. Lauren, you bring a light into this world and my life that I am eternally grateful for. Your taste is impeccable and impacts everyone. Catherine, you are belonging personified. You create space for everyone you encounter and invite them in with such grace and kindness. Peter B., you have changed my life in so many ways. Thank you for making everything better and smarter. Peter M., your thinking is infused throughout the pages and exercises. Your wisdom and counsel are seen throughout the words and exercises. I am grateful for you. Brooke, Jared, Kelsey, Jennifer, Caroline, Lydia, Raelyn, thank you for how you think and how you create solutions that no one else is thinking about. Blas, Jill Z., Mandy, Jennifer, Santi, Michelle, Jon, Karen, thank you for making everything come to life with such beauty and creating such deep connections with all who experience your talents. Stuart, thanks for your partnership and making Bermuda happen. John C., thanks for the foundation you set and friendship we keep. Caroline O., Skyler, and Charlie P., thank you for your research and the brilliance of the light you shine on the world. I cannot wait to see all you do in the years ahead. Thank you all for making Deutser, Deutser and for making the world a better, more accepting place. I love our beautiful mess.

There are so many friends and people who have demonstrated unwavering love and support. So many of you have been part of this journey with me and shared your thoughts and dreams. I am grateful for your friendship and your trust. Joe, thank you for your creativity, writing inspiration, and most of all your enduring kindness. Molly, thank you for being my trusted friend and valued partner. You have stretched me and helped me grow in so many ways. Wayne, you have always believed in me—as much as anyone at any time. Marc, you are a believer and someone who makes everyone feel like they belong. Adam, you were the first to let me know I fit. Andy, you have taught me to overcome, and you always do so with a smile. You each lead with an elegance and determination that inspires me. You have and continue to achieve at the highest levels. You have been there for me always, and I am forever grateful. There are so many friends who truly inspire me to think and dig deeper and so many others who patiently listen and who willingly share. Thank you all. And, to the Boys of Greylock Camp you hear so much about. And, why not! This is one of the most inspirational group of men that I know. We have shared and you have taught me even more. I am proud to share what we experienced firsthand with Bert, Irv, and Bernie. Bernie, you have been there for us and with us all these years. Gary, I think about you every day. Danny, your friendship, brilliance, and absolute kindness fill my soul and my life. Todd, you have been with me every step of the way, and I love all we have and continue to share. The generational love continues. Michael, you are the leader among leaders. I learn from you and your amazing successes, and I truly cherish our friendship. Jason, we share everything. And you are one of the greatest and most brilliant blessings in my life. I cannot think of a better friend, partner, business dreamer, or brother. Jared, I have loved how our friendship has evolved and am amazed by your calm, steady leadership. The list goes on and on . . . but Matt L., Dave, and so many others inspire me with your leadership and friendship. Barry M., thank you for reminding me that freedom is not free and that I can be an entrepreneur. Richard A., thank you for making the world healthier and better for everyone, especially me. Helen and Johnnie Mae, I am what I am because of you. Terri B., thank you for the gift of mindfulness and your friendship. Your ideas and spirit are and cherish our conversations, friendship, and changing the world together. LaToya, #woobie. Your grace under fire and amazing heart are a gift to the world. Never stop being you. Cloteal, thank you for inviting me in and keeping me there. Quan, you are an inspiration to me and true agent of change. Kyanna, thank you for teaching me the spirit of forgiveness. Chris D., your energy and passion are unmatched. Every ninety days a big win! You always deliver. Amalia, your leadership and brilliance know no bounds. Anne, thank you for believing and for doing all you do for everyone else. Kris, your brilliant and inviting leadership and genuine goodness inspire me. Tom A., thank you for believing and seeing something magical. Tom K., you are a blessing in my life, and I am forever grateful. Lisa, your vision and desire to do good is unmatched. Thank you for letting us spread happiness with you. Mike D., you are a transformational leader in every way. Dr. Lane, thank you for showing me the power of perseverance and doing right. Priscilla, thank you for believing when you didn't have to. Kirk, thank you for saving lives and making the world better because of your leadership. Amanda, I don't know how you do all you do. But you make a difference to so many every single day. Humbled by our work together. Angel, grateful for your leadership, always. Kenny, thanks for trusting us with all you do. I am a huge fan of you and your leadership. And Ted, great leaders run in the family. Patrick, you make me proud. I cannot wait to see what you achieve ahead. Bill P., your generosity of spirit and brilliant mind are a gift to all. Mike K., I love learning from you and with you. You find ways to win—no matter what is happening around you. Susan L., I learn from you every day through your kindness. Christy S., you are an inspiring leader. Keep being you! Dwayne, your leadership and calming influence are spectacular. David M., thank you for trusting and bringing us in to work with you and your brilliant leadership. Kelly, your generosity, thoughtfulness, and leadership have no bounds. Cal and Hannah, you trusted me in your most challenging moments. I see firsthand the amazing leadership and thoughtful change that you bring to your team and our community. Grateful. Greg, you are a the University of Texas, Rice University, and Stanford University, thank you for your willingness to share and trust. You make us all smarter and more aware. There are so many others who shared their words, thoughts, dreams, and brilliance. I am grateful to you all.

It is hard to write a book like this and not want to include every person who has touched my life and invited me inside. So, for all listed and all who were not, you are in my heart, and I am forever touched by you. Keep being open to what can be, and keep inviting people inside. Belonging rules!

SELECTED BIBLIOGRAPHY

Introduction

Bilotta, Isabel, Brad Deutser, and Brent Furl. *The Power of Belonging in the Workplace* (unpublished white paper). Deutser Clarity Institute.

Chapter 1

American Association for Access, Equity, and Diversity. "Affirmative Action Policies throughout History." Accessed January 30, 2023. www.aaaed.org/aaaed/History_of_Affirmative_Action.asp.

Melnick, R. Shep. "The Strange Evolution of Title IX Programs." *National Affairs*, summer 2018. www.nationalaffairs.com /publications/detail/the-strange-evolution-of-title-ix.

Ely, Robin J., Debra Meyerson, and Martin N. Davidson. "Rethinking Political Correctness." *Harvard Business Review*, September 2006. https://hbr.org/2006/09/rethinking-political-correctness.

Romano, Aja. "The Second Wave of 'Cancel Culture.'" *Vox*, May 5, 2021. https://www.vox.com/22384308/cancel-culture-free-speech -accountability-debate.

Roper, Cynthia. "Political Correctness." *Encyclopedia Britannica*, accessed January 30, 2023. www.britannica.com/topic/political -correctness.

Sullivan, Becky. "How the Supreme Court Has Ruled in the Past About Affirmative Action." *NPR*, November 1, 2022. www.npr.org/2022/11/01/1132935433/supreme-court-affirmative-action-history-harvard-admissions-university-carolina.

Vogels, Emily A., Monica Anderson, Margaret Portues, et al. "Americans and 'Cancel Culture': Where Some See Calls for Accountability, Others See Censorship, Punishment." *Pew Research*, May 19, 2021. www.pewresearch.org/internet/2021/05/19/americans-and-cancel-culture-where-some-see-calls-for-accountability-others-see-censorship-punishment/.

Chapter 2

Kim, Jennifer Y., and Loriann Roberson. "I'm Biased and So Are You. What Should Organizations Do? A Review of Organizational Implicit Bias Training Programs." *Consulting Psychology Journal* 74 (2021): 19–39. doi.org/10.1037/cpb0000211.

Chapter 3

Dvorak, Nate, and Bailey Nelson. "Few Employees Believe in Their Company's Values." Gallup, September 13, 2016. https://news.gallup.com/businessjournal/195491/few-employees-believe-company-values.aspx.

Chapter 4

Fadem, Terry. *The Art of Asking*. Hoboken, NJ: Pearson, 2009.

Eatough, Erin. "How Inclusive Leadership Impacts Your Entire Business." *BetterUp* (blog), February 25, 2021. www.betterup.com/blog/how-inclusive-leadership-impacts-your-entire-business.

Chapter 5

University of Illinois College of Agricultural, Consumer, and Environmental Sciences. "Are Leaders Born or Made? New Study

Shows How Leadership Develops." *ScienceDaily*, October 6, 2014. www.sciencedaily.com/releases/2014/10/141006133228.htm.

Chapter 6

Morelli, Peter, Brad Deutser, and Brent Furl. *Validating the Importance of Positivity in the Modern Workplace* (white paper). Deutser Clarity Institute, April 2020. https://deutser.com/writing/.

Oxford Languages. "Word of the Year 2016." Accessed January 30, 2023. languages.oup.com/word-of-the-year/2016/.

Society for Human Resources Management. "SHRM Study Reveals 20% of Workers Mistreated Due to Political Views." October 5, 2022. www.shrm.org/about-shrm/press-room/press-releases /pages/shrm-study-reveals-20-percent-of-workers-mistreated -due-to-political-views.aspx.

Suttie, Jill. "The Ripple Effects of a Thank You." *Greater Good Magazine*, December 20, 2019. https://greatergood.berkeley.edu /article/item/the_ripple_effects_of_a_thank_you.

United Nations. "Rise of Disinformation a Symptom of 'Global Diseases' Undermining Public Trust: Bachelet." *UN News*, June 28, 2022. news.un.org/en/story/2022/06/1121572.

Chapter 7

Eurich, Tasha. "What Self-Awareness Really Is (and How to Cultivate It)." *Havard Business Review*, January 4, 2018. www.hbr.org /2018/01/what-self-awareness-really-is-and-how-to-cultivate-it.

Chapter 8

Grant, Adam. "There's a Name for the Blah You're Feeling: It's Called Languishing." *New York Times*, April 19, 2021. www.nytimes .com/2021/04/19/well/mind/covid-mental-health-languishing .html.

INDEX

ABOUT THE AUTHOR

Photo by Jeff Fitlow

Brad Deutser is known for coaching and leading leaders through his company, Deutser, an innovative consultancy that designs a human approach to change. Brad works where most people feel uncomfortable and try to avoid. He is known for actively seeking out challenging and charged environments, as well as societal and politically sensitive ones. Creating spaces for belonging and initiating constructs to expand leadership in a more human, connective way has been the focus of his work for decades.

Brad's clients and coaching take him to amazing places—in athletics, aviation, education, entertainment, energy, finance, health care, nonprofit—with incredibly thoughtful leaders around the world. He takes on the most high-level challenges, forging through them with creativity and grace to design and bring to life the most original solutions. Brad has been called on to define and transition the culture at the NFL's Houston Texans as well as supporting the transformation of the University of Arizona football program, while serving as a leadership and performance coach to the players as well as executives across the world. He serves as the architect of the Wolff Center for Entrepreneurship at University of Houston, the three-time recognized #1 entrepreneurial program in the United States. The University of Texas selected his approach to navigate complex social and cultural issues. And countless leaders have brought the Deutser team in to navigate generational transitions and conflicts within families and complex companies, to facilitate cultural integration post-merger/acquisition, and to support the health, well-being, and safety of tens of thousands of employees across too many businesses to name.

Brad's first book, *Leading Clarity*, a national bestseller, is used by organizations to redefine their future and amplify their results. There is an indelible entrepreneurial spirit and passion for people that is evident in Brad and everything he does. One of his greatest passions is to design and create spaces for human connection, which is a hallmark of his work.

Follow Brad at
- LinkedIn @BradDeutser
- Twitter @BradDeutser
- bdeutser@deutser.com
- www.deutser.com
- www.instituteforbelonging.com